100 Military Leaders

Who Shaped World History

Samuel Willard Crompton

A Bluewood Book

This edition produced and published in 1999 by Bluewood Books
A Division of The Siyeh Group, Inc.,
P.O. Box 689
San Mateo, CA 94401

ISBN 0-912517-33-6

Printed in U.S.A.
10, 9, 8, 7, 6, 5, 4, 3, 2, 1

Edited by Lee A. Schoenbart
and Heidi Marschner
Copy Edited by Greg Aaron
Designed by David Price
Proofread by Gerry Hall

Key to cover illustration:
Clockwise, starting from top left:
Bernard Montgomery, Constantine the Great, George Washington, Napoleon Bonaparte, Joan of Arc, Simón Bolívar, Julius Caesar, and William Sherman in the center.

About the Author:
Samuel Willard Crompton teaches American and European history at Holyoke Community College. Crompton's other books include: *100 Americans Who Shaped American History* (Bluewood, 1998), *100 Battles That Shaped World History* (Bluewood, 1997), *100 Wars That Shaped World History* (Bluewood, 1997), *Gods and Goddesses of Classical Mythology* (Barnes and Noble, 1998) and *Presidents of the United States* (Smithmark, 1992)

Crompton holds degrees from Framingham State College and Duke University. He grew up and lives in western Massachusetts.

Picture Acknowledgements:
Bluewood Archives: all pages except: British Museum: 40, 54; Imperial War Museum: 90, 91, 100; Israel Information Agency: 35, 106; Library of Congress: 76, 77, 87, 103, 104; National Archives: 78, 82, 83, 84, 85, 86, 88, 92, 93, 98, 99, 101, 105, NYPL: 25, 30, 36, 53, 72; U.S. Army: 94, 107; U.S. Naval Institute: 80, 89, 95, 96, 97

TABLE OF CONTENTS

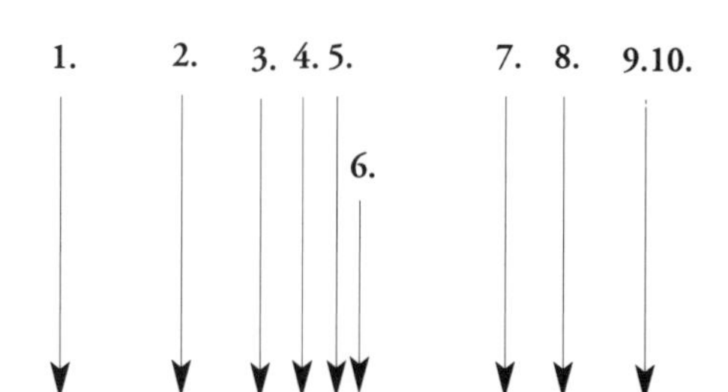

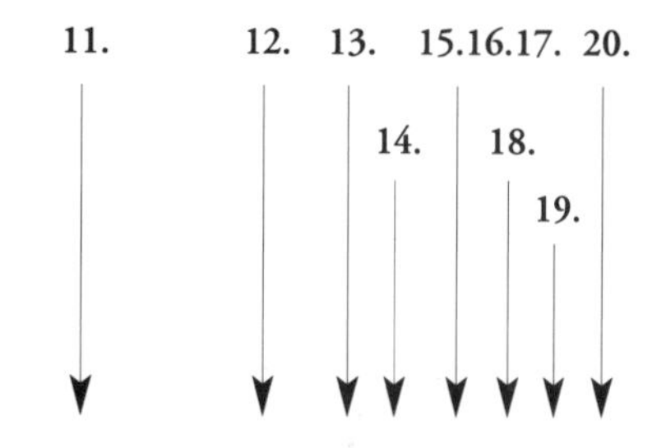

600 B.C. **A.D. 750**

TABLE OF CONTENTS

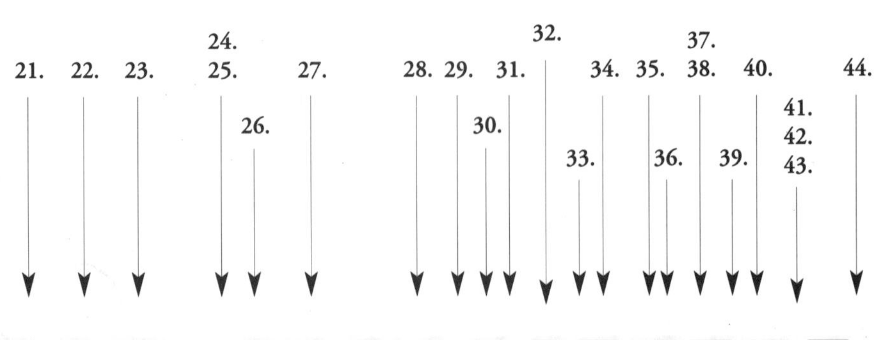

A.D. 751 **1500**

TABLE OF CONTENTS

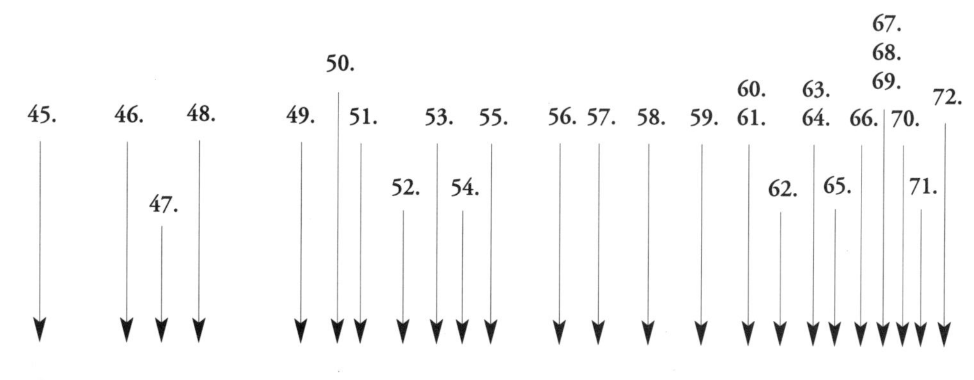

1501 **1800**

TABLE OF CONTENTS

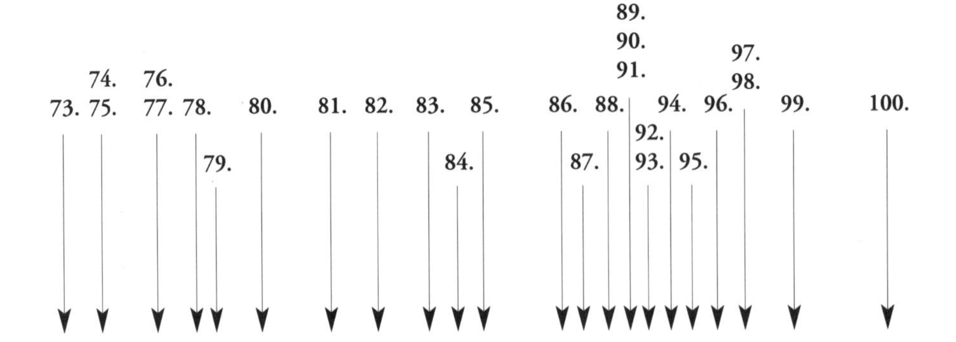

INTRODUCTION

"I can't spare this man, he fights." This was the reply of Abraham Lincoln when he was pressured by his friend Alexander Kelly McClure to replace Ulysses S. Grant as the Union army commander after the bloody battle of Shiloh in 1862. Lincoln had endured a succession of mediocre and timid military leaders during the first year of the Civil War. The president felt he had finally found in Grant a general who would wage the war in an uncompromising fashion. Instinctively, Lincoln knew he must support Grant.

Grant's relentless pursuit of victory was the key trait he shared with most of history's great military leaders. Whether they fought for gold (like Pizarro), glory (like Napoleon), national independence (like Joan of Arc) or religion (like Jan Zizka), great commanders have always exhibited an almost obsessive desire for victory.

What are some of the other characteristics of the great military leaders? What common ground can be found among people as different as Charlemagne, Cromwell and Chiang Kai-shek? All-consuming ambition is usually one answer people offer. Some assume that great military leaders would ruthlessly sacrifice anyone and everything to obtain their goals. Certainly that is true in some cases. Attila the Hun and Mao Zedong never worried about their casualty lists, but others, notably Nathanael Greene and Erwin Rommel, hated to lose any of their soldiers.

Even if ambition is something these 100 military leaders shared, then it must be stressed that some of them fought for larger and more selfless causes. Joan of Arc was ambitious for Dauphin Charles of France; he abandoned her nevertheless. Simón Bolívar dedicated his entire life to freeing South America, only to find that a united new country was beyond his reach. Vo Nguyen Giap labored tirelessly for 30 years to bring about an independent Republic of Vietnam.

What about the battlefield itself? Is there a fighting style that all these individuals shared? The answer is no. Some of them were brilliant improvisers, Chief Joseph and Garibaldi come to mind, while others like Bernard Montgomery and William T. Sherman were methodical planners.

Can we name the greatest of the great? Comparisons are difficult because weapons and tactics have changed so much over the centuries. Nevertheless, it is perhaps possible to create a "top 10" list. Each of these leaders probably had their own ideas about what makes a great military leader.

Napoleon once stated his ideas in this way, "What makes a good general? The answer is those qualities that serve a man well in public life: acumen, shrewdness, mental finesse, administrative ability, eloquence, not the eloquence of a lawyer but the eloquence that rouses an army. These are all civilian qualities and the general who is successful is the general who has them all."

Grant, we must admit, lacked many of Napoleon's requirements. Grant failed at business in the early part of his life. He was not eloquent. He had a dismal record as president of the United States. What Grant did possess to a supreme degree was firmness of purpose and intention. This trait gave him the nickname of "Unconditional Surrender (U. S.)" Grant, a title he won after he sent a famous message to the Confederate commander of Fort Donelson on February 16, 1862: "No terms except an unconditional and immediate surrender can be accepted."

That special type of uncompromising determination is what best distinguishes the great military leaders from the average ones. Great military leaders have exerted their will and courage in ways that have shaped world history.

1. Cyrus the Great
(C. 600–530 B.C.)

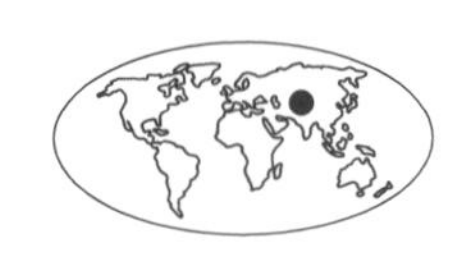

One of history's greatest warlords, **Cyrus** was born in what is the southern part of present-day Iran. Many stories have circulated regarding his parentage, but it seems most likely he was the son and grandson of men who ruled the region known as **Anshan**. Cyrus inherited the throne of Anshan and gathered the other tribes of the region called **Persis** (a present-day province of Fars, Iran). He led a revolt against his overlord, the Median king, **Astyages**. Joined by forces from the city of Babylon, Cyrus and his Persian warriors defeated the Medes. Cyrus entered the Median capital of **Ecbatana** (present-day Hamadan) and took the throne as king of **Persia**.

Two years after his entry to Ecbatana, Cyrus went to war against **Croesus**, the king of **Lydia** (present-day Turkey). Lydia had established the first known coinage system, and Croesus was reputed to be fabulously wealthy (hence, the old expression, "rich as Croesus"). The Lydian king consulted the Greek oracle at **Delphi**, which prophesied that if he attacked the Persians, a great empire would be destroyed. Never thinking that the empire the Oracle spoke of might well be his own, Croesus fought Cyrus. The Persians prevailed; Cyrus took Croesus prisoner and took the kingdom of Lydia and all its wealth for himself. In the following year, 546 B.C., the Ionian cities on the eastern coast of **Asia Minor** (Turkey) revolted against the Persians. Cyrus swiftly captured the cities, further expanding his empire.

Cyrus turned eastward in 545 B.C., taking his hard-riding Persian warriors all the way to the Indus River and the foothills of the Hindu Kush Mountains. He returned to Ecbatana and moved against Babylon, which had remained independent of his control. Cyrus captured the city, ending the Babylonian dynasty.

Cyrus the Great

The Persian king now controlled a vast empire stretching from the Indus River to the eastern shores of Asia Minor. He then cast an eager eye toward Egypt. Cyrus was prevented from marching eastward by attacks on the northern section of his empire. He marched north instead and met the nomadic Massagetai tribes in central Asia. There he was defeated and killed.

His concept of a world state lasted long after his death. The Persian cities of **Susa** and **Persepolis** stood at the center of the empire. The lands were connected by express riders who traveled on well-paved roads to carry news throughout the empire. Cyrus was buried at **Pasargadae** in a relatively simple tomb. A fierce warrior, but a benevolent and wise ruler, he was called "Father" by the Persians.

2. Themistocles

(C. 524–459 B.C.)

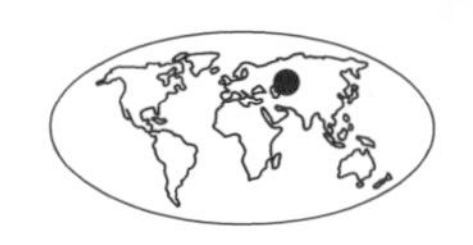

Heroic patriot, or double-dealing scoundrel? The debate continues about **Themistocles** (thehm-is-TOE-cleez), a native of Athens. He rose to become a champion of the lower classes in Athens, the Greek city that came close to developing a true democracy in the sixth century B.C. Themistocles became an ***archon*** (magistrate) in 493 B.C. He set about at once fortifying Piraeus, a naval port that was two miles away from the main city of Athens. He was one of 10 generals who led the Athenians at the **Battle of Marathon** (490 B.C.), where the first major threat from Persia was defeated on a rocky beach.

After the death of **Miltiades**, who had been first in command at Marathon, Themistocles became the dominant leader in Athens. He used the process of ostracism — political banishment — to rid the city of many of his political rivals. In 483 B.C., he persuaded the Athenians to build between 100 and 200 warships. Believing that Persia would strike again, Themistocles convinced the Athenians to cooperate with other Greek city-states in preparation for another war.

In 480 B.C., **Xerxes I** (ZERKS-eez), the Persian "King of Kings," led an enormous army and fleet to Greece. After winning the **Battle of Thermopylae**, Xerxes' troops entered Athens and found to their surprise that no one was there: the population had fled. Trusting in Themistocles (who had trusted in the Oracle at Delphi), the Athenians fled to nearby towns, while their sailors stood ready with their fleet at the Bay of Salamis.

Themistocles convinced his fellow Athenians to fight in the narrow bay, where the larger number of Persian ships would pose less of a threat. Following the lead of Themistocles, the Greeks fought and won an all-day naval battle that ended with the ruin of the Persian fleet. Lacking supplies that could only be brought in by water, Xerxes soon led his army in retreat, leaving the Greek city-states in freedom.

For some time, Themistocles was the greatest hero in Greece, but in 476 B.C., he was tried for cooperating with the Persians. Acquitted, he was nonetheless ostracized in 473 B.C. and had no choice but to flee Athens. Themistocles crossed the Aegean Sea to Ephesus in Asia Minor and presented himself to **Artaxerxes**, the new Persian king, and became a trusted advisor. The Persian leader gave him the town of Magnesia-on-the-Meadows to rule.

Themistocles, the Athenian politician and general who had changed sides in the last years of his life, had always covered his bases. It was later discovered he sent information to the Persians, even while he led the Athenian forces against them.

Battle of Salamis

3. Alcibiades
(c. 450–404 B.C.)

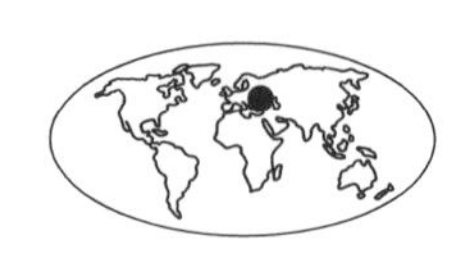

Alcibiades (al-sih-BY-ah-dees) was born in Athens, nephew to the great statesman **Pericles**, and briefly a disciple of the great philosopher **Socrates** (whose admonitions to seek balance and harmony were apparently wasted on the young man). Alcibiades became known for his disregard for any moral code.

After serving with distinction in the Athenian army (he saved Socrates' life at the **Battle of Delium** in 424 B.C.), Alcibiades was elected one of the 10 generals of Athens in 420 B.C. Pericles was dead, and the **Peloponnesian War** between Athens and Sparta was in its 12th year. Radically in favor of continuing the war, Alcibiades convinced his fellow military leaders to send a large force from the Athenian navy to attack the city of Syracuse (a Spartan ally) in Sicily. Named one of the fleet's commanders, Alcibiades fell into disgrace after images of the god Hermes were mutilated the night prior to departure. His political enemies persuaded the government that Alcibiades was responsible, and an escort was sent to bring him home.

Alerted to this danger, Alcibiades left the fleet and sailed to Argos. He then marched to Sparta, where he offered his services to his long-time enemies. Intrigued by the offer, the Spartan king allowed Alcibiades to remain. He was soon allowed to present himself to the king as a Spartan who valued only military skill and speaking the truth. Still, a traitor from any nation is generally viewed with distrust, and Alcibiades made the situation worse — by seducing the king's wife. Discovered, he fled from Sparta and crossed the Aegean Sea to Asia Minor, where he offered his services to **Tissaphernes**, the Persian ***satrap*** (governor).

Still hoping to return to Athens, Alcibiades made overtures that were rejected at first. Then a group of Athenian generals gave him command of an Athenian fleet based on the island of Samos. Departing quickly from the Persian court, Alcibiades took command and won several victories, notably at Cyzicus, where 60 Spartan ships were destroyed or captured. In 407 B.C., Alcibiades returned to Athens and was welcomed as a hero.

Alcibiades went into voluntary exile in Thrace, and the exile was soon made permanent by the end of the war. Sparta won a complete victory over Athens in 404 B.C., and the Spartan commander, **Lysander**, demanded the surrender of the man who had turned coat a total of three times. Alcibiades fled to Asia Minor, where the Persian satrap **Pharnabazus** agreed to allow him safe residence. Pressured by Lysander, Pharnabazus had Alcibiades slain by a group of armed men at his residence in Phrygia in the same year. Handsome, persuasive and unscrupulous, Alcibiades was finally brought down by his own double-dealing maneuvers.

Death of Alcibiades

4. Xenophon
(C. 430–355 B.C.)

A soldier and an author, **Xenophon** (ZEN-uh-fon) was born in Athens. He grew up in the tumult of the **Peloponnesian War**, and by the time of Athens defeat in 404 B.C., he was disillusioned by the politics of his home city. In 401 B.C., he accepted an offer to join the army of **Cyrus the Younger** (c. 424–401), a Persian prince who recruited 13,000 Greek mercenaries to fight with him against his older brother, King **Artaxerxes II** (ART-ah-ZERKS-eez).

Xenophon

The Persian-Greek troops marched from Lydia in Asia Minor to Babylonia, the land between the Tigris and Euphrates rivers (in present-day Iraq). Cyrus the Younger encountered no serious opposition until he met his brother's army on the plain at Cunaxa, 60 miles north of Babylon. The battle went well for the Greco-Persian forces, until Cyrus led a cavalry charge against his brother and was killed. Defeated and leaderless, the Greek mercenaries retreated from the field to consider their options.

Xenophon stepped into the debate and urged his fellows not to consider surrender. Why yield to the mercy of the enemy, he asked them, if they had a chance to make their way back to Greece? He became the leader of the mercenaries and guided them on their perilous retreat through 1,300 miles of hostile territory. The eight-month march involved many perils. The Greeks did not know the terrain, and they were the first large body of their countrymen to travel so deep into Asia. Xenophon led the Greeks past the ruins of **Nineveh**, which had been the capital of the **Assyrian Empire**. Although only 200 years had passed since the city's fall, Xenophon and his men had never heard of the city or its once-great people. The arduous journey was concluded when the vanguard of the Greeks called out "The sea! The sea!" They had reached Chrysopolis on the Sea of Marmara, directly across from Byzantium. Xenophon's leadership and tactics have been used as a model until the present time. In fact, he is seen as the inventor of the pattern of strategic retreat.

On his return to Greece, Xenophon learned that Athens had banished him. He therefore served with the Spartan army (399–394 B.C.) in its war with the Persian ***satrap*** (governor) of Asia Minor. Returning to Greece, Xenophon was given an estate by King **Agesilaus II** of Sparta.

During the next 20 years, Xenophon wrote 14 works. His best known works were *Hellenika* (seven volumes), a history of Greece that showed a pro-Spartan bias, *Cyrus' Anabasis* (seven volumes), and *Cyrus' Education* (eight volumes), an idealized biography of **Cyrus the Great**, founder of the Persian Empire (see no. 1). He moved to Corinth in 371 B.C., and his Athenian citizenship was restored in 369 B.C.

5. Philip II
(382–336 B.C.)

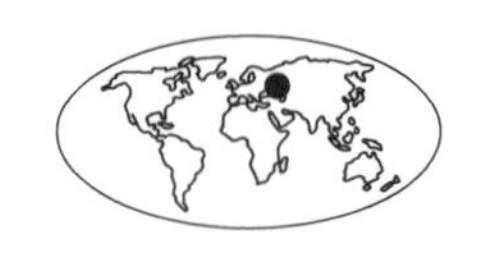

A younger son of King **Amyntas III**, **Philip** did not expect to attain the throne of **Macedonia**. Sent at an early age as a hostage to the Greek city-state of Thebes, he observed first-hand the military deployments of **Epaminondas**, the greatest Greek general of the time. Philip was returned to Macedonia by 359 B.C. Following the death of his older brother, **Perdiccas III**, he became king of Macedonia in his own right.

Philip turned the hard-riding, hard-drinking Macedonians into a formidable fighting force. He arrayed his farmer-soldiers in a phalanx, a tight rectangular battle formation. The soldiers in front held out long pikes, and the soldiers inside held their shields over their heads to protect the phalanx from arrows. To this tank-like formation, he added a corps of elite cavalry known as the **Companions**. These horsemen were used to terrify and overwhelm the enemy. Adding technology to the battlefield, he also employed catapults and siege towers. Philip fought side by side with his men, and he even lost his right eye in an early encounter, fighting against the Greek republic of Methone.

Philip II being shot in the right eye

Skillful in diplomacy as well as war, Philip first made sure that his throne was secure. He accomplished this by defeating the **Illyrians** in what later became Yugoslavia (358 B.C.) and taking the towns on the east coast of Macedonia. After expanding eastward into Thrace, Philip turned south and declared a "sacred war" against Thessaly. Actually, the only thing sacred to Philip was the gaining of territory and prestige.

Seeing the menace Macedonia posed to Greek freedom, the Athenian orator **Demosthenes** tried feverishly to stir up public sentiment against Philip. Demosthenes' efforts came too late; Athens declared war on Philip in 340 B.C. without having made adequate preparations. In 338 B.C., Philip and his 18-year-old son **Alexander** (see no. 6) met the Athenian and Theban forces on the field at Chaeronea in Boeotia. Prince Alexander led a spectacular charge of the Companions that won the day for Macedonia. Philip left garrisons in both Thebes and Corinth, but he declined to do so in Athens. Master of northern Greece, Philip forced all the Greek city-states except Sparta to join the **League of Corinth**, with himself as the leader.

Philip intended to attack the Persian province of Asia Minor (Turkey). The Athenian orator and teacher **Isocrates**, who saw in Philip the leader Greece needed, supported the plan. Family circumstances prevented Philip from carrying out his plans, though.

The greatest soldier of his day, and a true state-builder, Philip would be succeeded by his son, who would surpass his formidable achievements.

6. Alexander the Great
(356–323 B.C.)

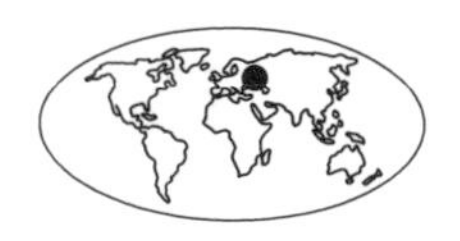

Born in Pella, Macedonia, **Alexander** was the son of King **Philip II** (see no. 5) and **Olympias**, an Epirean princess. He studied under the Greek philosopher **Aristotle**, and from an early age, showed both a keen mind and a talent for leadership. Alexander came of age at the **Battle of Chaeronea** (338 B.C.), where he led the Macedonian cavalry in a charge that swept the Athenians and Thebans from the field.

Alexander became king of Macedonia after the death of his father in 336 B.C.

In the spring of 334 B.C., Alexander and 35,000 battle-hardened troops crossed the Dardanelles into Asia Minor. He won his first engagement against the Persians at the Granicus River and proceeded to the city of **Gordium**, where he cut the famous **Gordian Knot**. The Gordian Knot was a knot of cornel bark tied around the yoke of a chariot. A legend had developed that the man who could untie the knot would become the ruler of all Asia. Alexander simply pulled out his sword and cut through the knot that had perplexed countless men before him.

Marching south he met the assembled army of **Darius III**, the King of Kings and the ruler of the Persian Empire. At the **Battle of Issus** (333 B.C.), Alexander used the mobility of his troops to confuse and defeat the much larger Persian army.

Alexander led his men into Lebanon and spent seven months reducing the Phoenician city of Tyre (TY-ree). He finally conquered that island city by building a causeway of earth and stones which still exists. He then went to Egypt, where high priests acclaimed him as a god. The Macedonian army left Egypt and marched into Persia proper, where Alexander fought and won a second great battle with Darius, this time at a site called Arabela (331 B.C.). Darius escaped from the field, was pursued with a vengeance, and finally fell at the hands of one of his own generals.

Alexander then devised a plan for "**homonoia**," to bring Greeks, Persians, and Macedonians together into one ethnic group. He married 10,000 of his soldiers to 10,000 Persian women in a one-day wedding ceremony for this purpose.

He brought his men all the way to the Indus River and fought a battle against Indian troops and their elephants (the first time the Greeks had faced such animals). Finally, in 326 B.C., Alexander's Macedonian soldiers demanded he lead them back to Persia. Angry, Alexander led them back by way of the harsh Gedrosian desert, where many lives were lost to hunger and thirst.

Alexander made his capital at Babylon where he died after a fever that was probably caused by drink. Since he left no male heir to succeed him, his vast empire was divided among his top generals. Greek became the common language of much of the Middle East and Hellenistic culture became dominant from Greece to the Tigris and Euphrates rivers.

Aristotle and his pupil Alexander

7. Hannibal
(c. 247–183 B.C.)

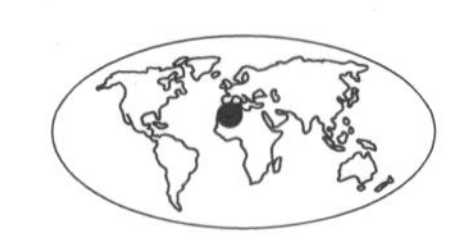

Son of **Hamilcar Barca, Hannibal** was born in Carthage, the great Phoenician city on the coast of North Africa. He was born during the **First Punic War** (264–241 B.C.), in which Rome defeated Carthage. After Rome took Sicily, Sardinia, and Corsica away from Carthage, Hamilcar Barca made his nine-year-old son swear his eternal hate for Rome.

Hannibal and his father went to Spain to establish a new Carthaginian empire. Following the death of his father and then of his brother-in-law, Hannibal became supreme commander in Spain and leader of the **Barcids** (the Barca family). Nervous about the rise of this new rival, Rome declared war on Carthage in 218 B.C., starting the **Second Punic War**.

Hannibal led 35,000 troops and a number of elephants over the Pyrenees and Alps. He lost nearly all the elephants and many of his troops to the frigid conditions in the Alps, but he recruited Gallic tribespeople to join his attack on Rome.

Having defeated Carthage in the First Punic War, the Romans were supremely confident. To their astonishment, Hannibal defeated them at the Ticinus River (218 B.C.) and the Trebia River (218 B.C.) and won a major victory at Lake Trasimene (217 B.C.). The **Battle of Cannae** (216 B.C.) was Hannibal's masterpiece. He lured the body of Roman infantrymen to the center of his own lines, then caught them completely unprepared when his cavalry swept around the wings and trapped them. Fifty thousand Romans perished that day.

Meanwhile, Roman armies led by **Publius Cornelius Scipio** (see no. 8) conquered Carthaginian Spain. Hannibal's brother **Hasdrubal** escaped from Spain with 10,000 men and reached northern Italy, having followed Hannibal's route over the Alps. However, Hasdrubal was caught by two Roman armies, and his force was destroyed.

Hannibal

Hannibal learned of his brother's efforts only when Hasdrubal's head was thrown into his camp.

In 203 B.C., Hannibal was recalled by Carthage to defend the city against the Roman army, led by Scipio. The **Battle of Zama** (202 B.C.) showed that Scipio and the Romans had successfully copied Hannibal's style in war. This time it was Hannibal and the Carthaginians who were caught in a vise between Roman infantry and cavalry.

Hannibal escaped from the field and persuaded the leaders of Carthage to seek peace. He retired to private life at the end of the war and served as a magistrate for the city in 196 B.C. His political foes in Carthage persuaded Rome that Hannibal was ready to fight once more. Rome demanded that Carthage surrender Hannibal, but he fled to the court of **Antiochus III** of Syria. Hannibal encouraged Antiochus to fight Rome, and the resulting **Roman-Syrian War** (192–189 B.C.) ended in complete victory for the Romans. Hannibal then fled to the court of **Prusias** of **Bithynia**, where he took poison rather than be taken prisoner by the Romans.

8. Publius Cornelius Scipio
(c. 233–183 B.C.)

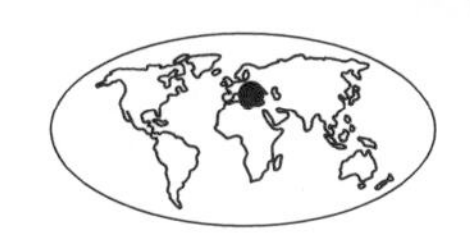

Born in Rome, **Scipio** (SHEEP-ee-oh) came from one of the city's most distinguished noble families. His father, who had the same name, was a Roman consul who fought against **Hannibal** (see no. 7) in northern Italy at the start of the **Second Punic War.** Scipio saved his father's life at the **Battle of Ticinus River** (218 B.C.) and rallied the remnants of the Roman army after the **Battle of Cannae** (216 B.C.).

Scipio admired Hannibal's success in battle. Studying the Carthaginian leader's battle tactics, he realized that the deployment of fast, light cavalry was the key to Hannibal's victories. Scipio persuaded the Roman Senate to let him open a second front, in Carthaginian Spain. He went to Spain as proconsul in 210 B.C. and captured Cartagena (New Carthage). Scipio revised traditional Roman tactics; he lightened the equipment of his men and trained them to maneuver quickly in a manner similar to that of the Carthaginians. Using this new style of war, Scipio consistently defeated the Carthaginians in Spain. By 206 B.C. he had won control of nearly the entire peninsula.

Scipio returned to Rome in 205 B.C. After long debate, he obtained the Senate's permission to take the war to Hannibal's homeland in North Africa. He took a Roman army across the Mediterranean in 204 B.C. and swiftly defeated two Carthaginian armies brought against him. He also earned the good will and alliance of **Masinissa**, a **Numidian** prince who brought additional cavalry to the Roman camp.

In 202 B.C., Scipio met Hannibal on the plains of Zama. The battle was hard-fought, but Scipio defused the power of the Carthaginian lines by stampeding their elephants and catching them in a vise with Masinissa's cavalry behind them. The student had met the master and won.

Scipio dictated harsh terms of peace to Carthage, then returned to Rome. He was honored with a triumphal march through Rome and received the surname "Africanus." Many years later, he would be called **Scipio Africanus Major** to distinguish him from his grandson, who destroyed Carthage in the **Third Punic War** (149–146 B.C.) and was named **Scipio Africanus Minor.**

In 190 B.C., he served as legate to his brother **Lucius Scipio** who won a crushing victory over **Antiochus III** of Syria in the **Roman-Syrian War.** Returning to Rome, Scipio found himself and his brother accused of accepting bribes from Antiochus. The brothers were acquitted in a memorable trial, and Scipio retired to his villa at Liternum in Campania. Bitter over the trial and angry that his name had come under suspicion, he ordered that his remains be interred at Liternum, not conveyed to Rome. Rome's greatest soldier felt dishonored by an ungrateful public.

Scipio and Hannibal at Zama

9. Pompey the Great
(c. 106–47 B.C.)

It was **Pompey**'s misfortune that his great military victories were eclipsed by those of **Julius Caesar** (see no. 10). Born in Rome, the son of **Pompeius Strabo**, Pompey came from the aristocracy. In 83 B.C., he became a follower of **Lucius Cornelius Sulla**, a patrician who became the unofficial dictator of Rome. During the **Social Wars** between the followers of **Sulla** and those of **Caius** (KAI-us) **Marius**, Pompey won several victories in Italy and then crossed to Sicily and North Africa, where he defeated Marian forces. On his return to Rome, Pompey was honored with a triumph and awarded the title of "Magnus," or "Great."

Following Sulla's death in 78 B.C., the Roman Senate sent Pompey to Spain. He fought and defeated Marian rebels there. He returned to Italy just in time to defeat the remnants of an army of former slaves who had rebelled under the leadership of **Spartacus.** In point of fact, **Marcus Licinius Crassus** (c. 115–53 B.C.) had done most of the work of defeating the rebels; it was Pompey's good fortune to arrive at the moment when the rebellion's force had been spent.

In 67 B.C. the Senate gave Pompey supreme power at sea in order to deal with pirates in the Mediterranean who commanded a total of 1,000 galleys and 400 towns. A masterful organizer, Pompey defeated the pirates in four months by capturing their bases. This great success was followed by his campaign in Asia Minor against **Mithridates VI**, the king of **Pontus**. Pompey defeated Mithridates, then besieged and captured the Jewish capital of **Jerusalem**. When he returned to Rome in 62 B.C., Pompey was beyond doubt the greatest military leader in the Mediterranean world.

Pompey the Great

Pompey formed a triumvirate — a three-man government — with Crassus and Julius Caesar. In 54 B.C. Crassus was killed on a military expedition against the Parthians. Pompey became sole consul in 52 B.C., and he ordered Caesar to return to Rome without his army.

Caesar refused and instead invaded Italy. Pompey fled to Greece to assemble his forces there. The stage was set for a climactic showdown between the two greatest generals of the day. Pompey rebuffed Caesar's troops at the port of Dyrrhachium (present-day Durres, Albania) and then pursued his foe. The two armies clashed again at Pharsalus in 48 B.C. Pompey, who had the larger army, gambled everything on a massive cavalry attack against Caesar's right flank. When the assault failed, Caesar's troops, backed by German mercenaries on horseback, scattered Pompey's forces. Pompey escaped from Greece and went to Egypt where he was treacherously murdered by followers of King **Ptolemy XIII**.

10. Julius Caesar
(100–44 B.C.)

Possibly the greatest commander of all time, **Julius Caesar** thrived on war.

Born into an ancient patrician family, Caesar was nonetheless affiliated with the plebeian (commoner) followers of **Caius** (KAI-us) **Marius** in his youth. He rose swiftly in civil and religious authority, becoming **Pontifex Maximus** (high priest) in 63 B.C. However, his military skill was virtually unknown until 59 B.C. when he obtained the proconsulship of Cisalpine Gaul (the southern part of present-day France).

Caesar quickly astonished those who thought they had known the extent of his talents. He conducted a campaign against the Helvetii in present-day Switzerland (58 B.C.) and nearly annihilated the tribe. Asked by some of the chieftains of southern Gaul to repel German invaders, Caesar marched against **Ariovistus** and destroyed his army, pursuing the survivors to the Rhine River. Having involved himself in Gaul, Caesar slowly began to constrict the area of Free Gaul in an enormous circular vise grip. He campaigned against the Beglai (in modern-day Belgium) and sailed across the channel to Britain, where he carried out the first Roman invasion of that land. By 52 B.C., Caesar had most of Gaul within his grasp. That same year, the Arverni chief, **Vercingetorix**, organized a tribal confederacy and carried out a massive war against the Romans. Caesar escaped from several tight spots before he ended the war and captured Vercingetorix at the **Siege of Alesia**.

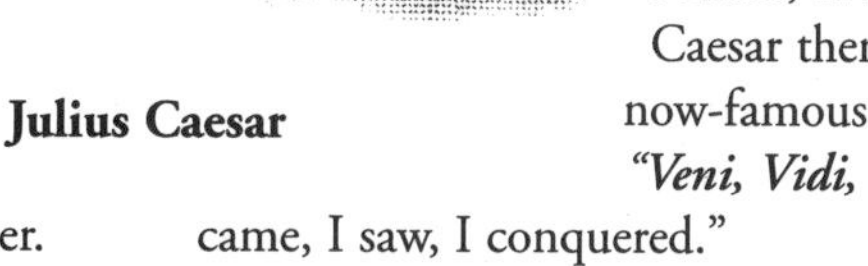

Julius Caesar

Summoned by his former political ally, **Pompey** (see no. 9), Caesar returned to Rome in January 49 B.C., but he did so at the head of his army. Pompey fled to Greece, where Caesar pursued him, and in 48 B.C., Caesar won a crushing victory over Pompey at the **Battle of Pharsalus.** Caesar pursued his foe to Egypt, where the followers of King **Ptolemy XIII** presented him with the head of Pompey. Caesar is said to have wept at the sight.

Caesar then joined forces with the Egyptian princess, **Cleopatra**, and they defeated her brother. Leaving Cleopatra on the throne of Egypt, Caesar went to Asia Minor, where he defeated **Pharnaces**, the son of **Mithridates** of Pontus, in five days. Caesar then stated the now-famous words, *"Veni, Vidi, Vici,"* or "I came, I saw, I conquered."

Caesar returned to Rome and was greeted with tremendous acclaim. He revised the Roman calendar (based on the calendar of Egypt) and reorganized the government. He seemed nearly ready to make himself emperor of Rome when he was struck down by a group of assassins on the floor of the Senate in 44 B.C. The Roman Republic had come to an end, and Caesar's nephew **Octavian** became the first true emperor of Rome.

11. Constantine the Great
(c. 280–337)

The man who made Christianity acceptable to Rome was born in Naissus in what later became Yugoslavia. **Flavius Valerius Aurelius Constantinus** was the son of **Constantius** and **Helena** (who later became a saint of the Catholic Church). Constantine grew up amid the turmoil caused by the division of leadership within the **Roman Empire**; there were two ***augusti*** (rulers), each with a ***caesar*** (governor) who ruled the **Eastern** and **Western Roman Empires**. Since his father was one of the two caesars, Constantine was sent as a hostage to the court of the other caesar, **Galerius**, a practice that was designed to ensure peace.

Constantine served ably against the Persians in Galerius' army. He then escaped from Galerius and joined his father in Gaul; the two went to Britain to fight the Picts. While they were there his father died, and Constantine was recognized as a new caesar.

Constantine

Galerius accepted Constantine as caesar of the lands north of the Alps, but further political tumult led to a civil war by A.D. 308. Constantine married Fausta, the daughter of a former augusti named **Maximian.** He later had to fight his brother-in-law **Maxentius**, the son of Maximian and brother of Fausta, for the throne. Prior to meeting Maxentius, he experienced a vision in which he was told he would conquer under the sign of the Christian cross.

Constantine won the **Battle of Milvian Bridge** (312). He entered the imperial city of Rome in triumph. He took care to disband the elite **Praetorian Guard**, which for centuries had made and unmade emperors before him.

As ruler of the Western Roman Empire, Constantine came into conflict with **Licinius,** who ruled the Eastern Roman Empire. The two men finally came to blows in A.D. 323; Constantine won a battle near **Adrianople** (present-day Greece) and became sole ruler of the empire.

As emperor, Constantine reorganized the Roman army. He recruited more cavalry troops and turned the army into more of a field force than a fortification-based one. The mobile troops he created allowed the empire to survive longer than it would have otherwise. Constantine also changed the imperial capital; he had the city of **Constantinople** built where Greece and Turkey meet.

Most importantly, Constantine changed imperial policy toward the Christian minority within the empire. The **Edict of Milan** (A.D. 313) abolished the official persecution of Christians. Constantine presided over the **Council of Nicaea** (A.D. 325) which established the official **Nicaean Creed of the Church**; it declared that God the Father, God the Son, and the Holy Spirit were inseparable from one another. All Christians who failed to follow this doctrine were labeled heretics. Constantine fully accepted Christianity himself, just prior to his death.

12. Alaric the Goth
(c. 370–410)

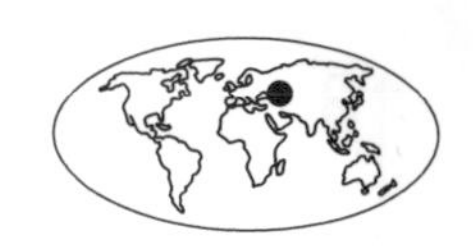

Alaric, the warlord who captured Rome was born on the island of Peuce, at the mouth of the Danube River in present-day Romania. In A.D. 390, he led a group of Visigothic tribespeople south against the **Eastern Roman Empire**, centered at **Constantinople**. Alaric's advance was stopped by Roman troops under the command of **Flavius Stilicho**, who was from the Vandal tribe.

Alaric attacked Greece in A.D. 395. His Gothic soldiers ravaged the major cities and destroyed the **Temple of Demeter**. Only bribes offered by the Eastern Roman emperor placated Alaric, who then withdrew. The emperor gave Alaric the title of ***magister militum*** (master of the soldiers) and allowed him to control **Illyricum** in what later became Yugoslavia. The latter gift was a mistake, since Alaric soon used Illyricum as a base from which to harass the **Western Roman Empire**, centered in Rome. Alaric invaded Italy in A.D. 401 and again in A.D. 402–403. Both times he was repulsed by Stilicho who forced him to retreat to Illyricum.

Stilicho was murdered in A.D. 408. Lacking his skillful leadership, Rome and Italy lay open to future invasions. Alaric invaded Italy again and twice laid siege to Rome itself. Both times, he accepted tribute payments from the city and withdrew his troops, although he forced the Romans to elect a puppet emperor who then named Alaric commander-in-chief of the Roman forces. This confusing situation was typical of the Roman Empire during its last 50 years as Romans and barbarians commingled throughout the empire.

In A.D. 410, the Roman emperor sanctioned a surprise attack on Alaric's camp. Furious by this betrayal, Alaric moved on Rome and commenced his third siege of the Eternal City. After three weeks of inconclusive fighting, treachery delivered the city to Alaric. The Salarian Gate was opened, and the Goths poured into the city, ravaging the buildings and monuments for three days. When news of this attack spread to other parts of the empire, many people were stunned. Rome, which had held itself in power and grandeur, had not been taken for more than 800 years, since the Gauls had done so in 390 B.C.

Alaric marched south from Rome. He wanted to move his tribe to North Africa, but his fleet was driven back to port by a major storm. He died suddenly, just months after the assault on Rome, and was buried at a secret location on the Busento River in southern Italy. His men killed the slaves who had buried him so that no one would find and desecrate the grave.

Alaric the Goth

13. Attila the Hun
(c. 406–453)

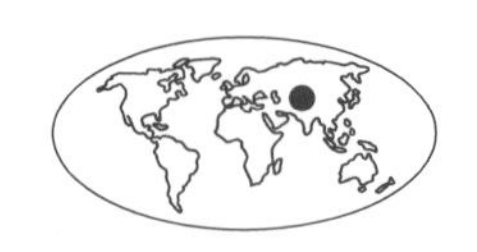

No military name conjures up as much sheer terror as that of **Attila the Hun**. The Huns were a warlike, nomadic people from Central Asia who swept into the Black Sea and Danube River regions around A.D. 370. Their violent arrival displaced many of the Visigothic and Ostrogothic tribespeople, who were less of a threat to Rome than the Huns.

Attila battles the Visigoths

In A.D. 433, he and his brother **Bleda** jointly inherited leadership of the tribe from their uncle. The Huns, who had already experienced success, were receiving an annual tribute payment of 700 pounds of gold from the **Eastern Roman Empire** in **Constantinople**. Attila was occupied at first with cementing his control over the area around the Danube. Then he turned his attention to the Eastern Roman Empire.

Attila led an invasion of the eastern **Balkan provinces** in A.D. 441. Because many of the Roman soldiers were away in Sicily, he advanced rapidly and won concessions from the emperor. Attila raised the annual tribute to 2,100 pounds of gold and withdrew to the Danube. He had his brother Bleda killed around A.D. 445 and became sole leader of the Hunnish nation.

The Huns returned to the offensive in A.D. 447. Attila led his mounted troops in a campaign that was stopped only at Thermopylae in Greece. Attila then turned east and went all the way to Constantinople, where he was halted. Even the ferocity of his men could not overawe the Romans, safe behind the great walls of the city.

Deciding to attack the **Western Roman Empire**, Attila raised an enormous army composed of Huns, Ostrogoths, Gepids, Heruli, and Alan tribespeople. He led them west into Gaul in A.D. 451. There his army clashed with forces led by Roman general **Aetius** and Visigothic king **Theodoric**. The two armies collided at the **Battle of Chalons**. Although King Theodoric was killed in the fighting, the Huns and their allies suffered heavy losses.

In A.D. 452, Attila invaded northern Italy. The Huns pillaged several northern Italian cities and seemed poised to march on Rome itself when Attila received a diplomatic visit from Pope **Leo I**. The substance of their conversation remains a mystery. It is an indisputable fact that afterward Attila ceased his march and, with his army, left Italy. The great question remains — did Pope Leo persuade Attila to do so, or did the lack of food for his horses convince Attila to retire?

Attila died in A.D. 453. Popular legend claims he burst a blood vessel on the night of his wedding to the Gothic maiden, Hilda. Deprived of his leadership, the Huns broke into smaller groups and their nation never regained the prominence it had held under Attila, the terror of the western world.

14. Clovis of the Franks
(c. 466–511)

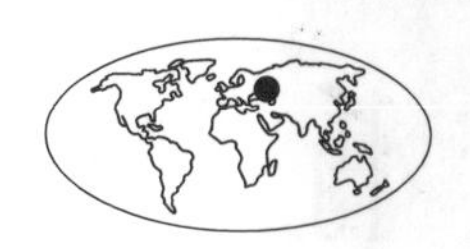

Roman Gaul disintegrated into sets of small barbarian kingdoms around A.D. 400, but one man reunited them, a Gaulish leader named **Clovis of the Franks.** Little is known of Clovis' youth. His father was **Childeric,** leader of the **Salic Franks** in northeastern Gaul. Childeric died in A.D. 481, and Clovis took his position.

Clovis wanted to expand his tribal lands. First, he turned east and defeated the Thuringian tribe in A.D. 491. Then he looked south and married Clotilda, niece of the two brothers who were joint kings of Burgundy. The marriage had an unexpected effect because Clotilda was a Christian. Slowly, she worked to convert Clovis. He allowed their children to be baptized as Christians, but held off himself until A.D. 496. In that year, Clovis fought the Swabian tribe in an important battle at Tolbiac. Prior to the battle, he prayed to the Christian god and promised he would convert to Christianity if he won. Clovis did triumph, and he became a Christian. He also required some 3,000 of his followers to do the same.

Clovis' feelings were said to be a combination of barbarian vengeance and Christian pathos after repeatedly hearing the story of the crucifixion of Christ. "Had I been present with my valiant Franks," Clovis was alleged to exclaim, "I would have revenged his injuries."

Around A.D. 506, Clovis had permanently subdued the Swabians. He then turned his attention south once more and launched a series of campaigns against the Visigothic tribes that held power in southern France. He won a major battle against them at Vouille in A.D. 507, and soon all of southern Gaul (with the exception of present-day Provence) was in his hands.

His victories brought Clovis widespread attention. The Byzantine emperor in Constantinople, **Anastasius I,** gave him the honorary title of Roman consul and encouraged him to make war on the Ostrogothic kingdom of Italy, led by King **Theodoric.** Clovis did just that, but his campaign (A.D. 509–510) yielded him little glory and no expansion of his territory.

Clovis died in Paris on November 27, A.D. 511. At that time, Gaul was largely united, due to his ceaseless efforts. However, his achievement was soon blunted; his four sons divided the kingdom amongst themselves. Clovis left three important legacies to the future kingdom of France: he created the **Merovingian** dynasty, which lasted until A.D. 751; he made Orthodox Christianity the official religion of his people; and he created an alliance with the papacy in Rome that would outlast even his own dynasty.

Clovis

15. Belisarius
(c. 505–565)

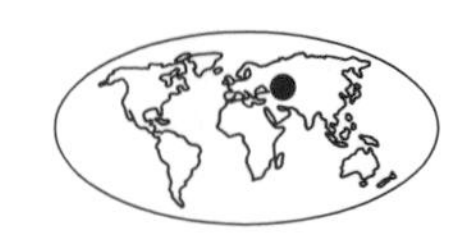

The greatest soldier of the **Byzantine Empire** was born in Germane, Ilyria (il-IR-ee-ah), in what later became Yugoslavia. **Belisarius** served in the imperial bodyguard in **Constantinople** and developed a lifelong loyalty to Emperor **Justinian I.** Belisarius was given command of the Byzantine army in the **Byzantine-Persian War**. He defeated the Persians at Daras in A.D. 530, but was himself defeated at Callinicum, Syria, in A.D. 531. This was the only outright loss of his career.

Belisarius was recalled to Constantinople, where he put down the **Nika Revolt** (A.D. 532), which would otherwise have cost Justinian his throne. In A.D. 533, Justinian sent Belisarius to North Africa to begin a series of campaigns that both men hoped would restore lands the empire had lost to the tribes there.

Belisarius

Belisarius conducted a brilliant campaign in Africa. With only 16,000 soldiers, he cleared all of North Africa of the Vandal tribe and brought King **Gelimer** to Constantinople as a prisoner. Thrilled by this success, Justinian sent his trusted soldier to fight in Sicily and Italy. Commanding only 8,000 men, Belisarius recovered Sicily and southern Italy. His greatest single success came in A.D. 536, when he entered the city of Rome. The greatest city of the ancient world had fallen to numerous attacks since A.D. 410, but Belisarius had now reclaimed it. It appeared as if a new era were dawning, one that would reunite the **Eastern and Western Roman Empires.**

Within weeks of his entry into Rome, Belisarius was besieged by a large Ostrogothic army. He withstood the siege, which lasted until A.D. 538, then he marched north and captured Ravenna, the Ostrogothic capital. Belisarius was recalled to Constantinople and quickly sent eastward to fight against the Persians. He repulsed their attack on Asia Minor in A.D. 542 and was transferred again to Italy. On this, his second mission to the Italian peninsula, Belisarius made only slow progress, and in A.D. 548 he asked to be recalled to Constantinople.

He came out of retirement to repel the Bulgar tribe, which threatened Constantinople in A.D. 559. In A.D. 563, he was accused of conspiring against the emperor. The great Byzantine commander died, probably in Constantinople, in A.D. 565. Belisarius' conquests were soon undone by other invasions, but his achievement had been substantial during his lifetime. He was, beyond doubt, the most effective commander to ever lead the Byzantine armies.

16. Khalid ibn al-Walid
(?–642)

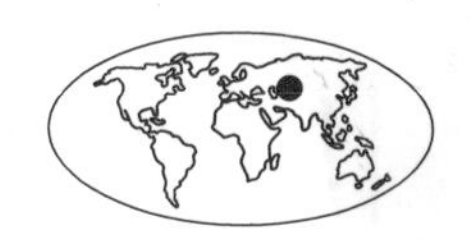

One of the greatest military leaders to follow the standard of Islam, **Khalid ibn al-Walid** was actually a foe of **Mohammed** at the start of the prophet's ministry. Born into a noble family in **Mecca**, Khalid won the **Battle of Uhud** for the enemies of Mohammed through a series of surprise attacks. By A.D. 628 or 629, Khalid switched sides and became a fervent believer in Mohammed and the Islamic faith. The reasons for his turnaround are unknown; it is possible he was swept up by the outpouring of religious fervor that attended the last three years of Mohammed's life.

Khalid led an unsuccessful attack on the Byzantine frontier in A.D. 630; upon his return, Mohammed named him "**Sword of God**" for his steadfastness in the difficult retreat. Khalid entered Mecca in triumph with Mohammed, and in A.D. 631, the prophet sent him to convert other Bedouin tribespeople on the Arabian peninsula.

Mohammed died in June A.D. 632, and a power struggle immediately broke out among rival leaders. Many Arabs choose to follow the "false prophet," **Musailima**. The true successor to Mohammed was the caliph king, **Abu Bekr**. He sent Khalid on a military mission to quell the followers of Musailima. Khalid followed his orders with a vengeance. He directed the **Battle of Akraba**, where Musailima and most of his followers were killed. Khalid waged a pitiless campaign that totally overwhelmed the rebel tribes of Asad, Tamin, Ghatafani, and Hanifa. By the middle of A.D. 633, the entire Arabian peninsula lay at the feet of Abu Bekr and the followers of Mohammed.

Khalid paused only briefly before pushing on to the Euphrates River to wage war against Persian forces. To his surprise, and the surprise of scholars today, the Persians gave way rapidly before his assaults. Within one year, he was master of the entire Euphrates area. Khalid had few diversions or amusements; he lived to fight.

Ordered to further his conquests, Khalid pushed northwest to Syria and made rapid headway against the Byzantine armies there. His greatest triumph came in A.D. 634, when he entered the venerable city of Damascus, having spread Islam far more rapidly than anyone expected. His fortunes changed, however, when Abu Bekr died that same year. The new caliph immediately removed Khalid from overall command of the Arab forces. Instead, he was given a subordinate position in the Syrian campaign, in which he captured the city of Homs.

Khalid later served as governor of part of Syria, but never regained his former prominence. He died in A.D. 642, either in Medina or Homs, and his tomb was consecrated in Homs.

View of Damascus

17. Tariq ibn Ziyad
(?–700)

The man for whom **Gibraltar** is named was a **Berber**, probably born in North Africa. Nothing is known of **Tariq**'s early years. He first appeared in the historical record as a Berber and former slave who was appointed a subordinate by **Musa ibn Nusayr** (c. A.D. 660–c. 714), the Arab governor of Morocco. Tariq was left in charge of the city of Tangier.

In A.D. 710, an Arab reconnaissance party crossed the narrow body of water between North Africa and Spain, called the "**Pillars of Hercules**" by the Greeks and Romans. The Arabs found Spain to be weak and reported this to Tariq. The Berber leader decided to see for himself, and on April 27, A.D. 711, he crossed the Pillars of Hercules with 7,000 soldiers, nearly all of them Berber tribespeople rather than Arabs. Tariq landed near a large rock that jutted out from the coast of Spain; that rock was named "**Jebel Tariq**" (Tariq's Rock). The Spanish later converted those words to "Gibraltar."

Berbers

Tariq soon discovered that his scouts had been correct. Visigothic Spain was divided and offered little resistance to the invaders. Tariq rapidly advanced northward, and on July 19, A.D. 711, he fought the **Battle of La Janda** against the army of King **Roderick**, the last Christian king of Visigothic Spain. Tariq won the battle and moved on to occupy the Visigothic capital of Toledo.

Learning of his lieutenant's success, Musa crossed the Pillars of Hercules with 18,000 troops (most of them Arabs) in June A.D. 712. He met Tariq at Talavera and scolded his subordinate for having traveled so far and conquered so much without orders to do so. By this time, the last Visigothic nobles had fled to the mountain region of Asturias in northern Spain, the area that would later become the center of the Christian kingdoms of Leon, Castile and Navarre.

Tariq and Musa had pushed the Christians out of southern and central Spain, further expanding the area of the world under the sway of Islam.

Musa was summoned by the caliph of Damascus to return east and report on the conquest. Musa and Tariq went to Damascus together, bringing a large convoy of prisoners. They reached Syria in February A.D. 715. Caliph al-Walid lay dying, and his successor showed no gratitude to either Musa or Tariq for their conquests. The two men ended their lives in complete obscurity in the East. They never returned to Spain, most of which they had conquered under the banner of Mohammed.

18. Leo III, the Isaurian
(c. 680–741)

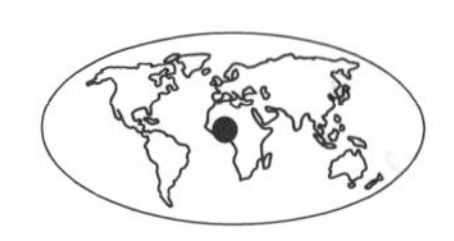

Destined to be the leader who sustained the **Byzantine Empire**, **Leo** was born in Germanicia in northern Syria to a noble family. He moved with his family to Thrace, on the eastern side of the Sea of Marmara, where Europe and Asia come together. As a young man, Leo assisted Byzantine emperor **Justinian II** in his attempt to recover the throne from a usurper. Not only was the Byzantine Empire divided internally, but it faced an enormous threat from the Arab forces that had recently conquered most of the Middle East, including Leo's homeland in Syria.

Justinian rewarded Leo with the title of ***spartharius*** and sent him on a diplomatic mission to the Caucasus Mountains, but the mission was frustrating and accomplished little. Following the death of Justinian II, Leo was made governor of the Anatolikonm province, the largest in Asia Minor (present-day Turkey).

Leo led the opposition to **Theodosius III** and was crowned emperor in his own right in A.D. 717. It was fortunate for the Byzantine Empire that its new leader had a military background, since the Arabs descended on the capital city, **Constantinople**, that very summer. The Arab leader, **Maslama**, brought an enormous fleet and army to the area and placed the city under siege.

The year-long siege (A.D. 717–718) was a fiercely fought contest. Leo battled back with the use of "**Greek fire**," a combination of sulfur and lime that set fire to enemy ships. Leo also employed his knowledge of the terrain and geography to outmaneuver and confuse his foes. Still, the Arabs came close to victory, and only the severe winter of A.D. 717–718 prevented the fall of the city. When Maslama and his fleet departed in the summer, minus thousands of men and hundreds of ships, the Islamic armies lost their best chance to destroy the Byzantine Empire.

Leo celebrated the victory and kept his people busy building even stronger defenses around the city. He need not have worried; the Arabs did not return in his lifetime, and the future sieges of Constantinople would be carried out by Seljuk Turks and Ottoman Turks, not by Arabs.

Famous in his later years, Leo carried out a campaign against icon worship within the empire. He died in A.D. 741, confident that his victories had enabled the empire to withstand many foes, both internal and external. The dynasty he founded lasted until A.D. 802. It has often been called the "**Isaurian Dynasty**," but it should properly be called the Syrian dynasty.

Use of "Greek fire"

19. Charles Martel
(689–741)

Known as "**Charles the Hammer,**" **Charles Martel** is famous for his defeat of the Arabs at Poitiers in A.D. 732. He was an illegitimate son of **Pepin of Heristal**, mayor of the palace of the Merovingian kingdom of the Franks. Following his father's death, Martel was imprisoned by his father's widow, who did not want any rivals to her family line.

Charles escaped from prison, raised an army of Austrasians, and defeated the Neustrian army. He became the sole "mayor of the palace" in A.D. 723. By this time, the Merovingian dynasty had declined through intermarriage, and the mayor of the palace conducted the true business of the kingdom, though he lacked the title of king.

Martel led campaigns against the Frisians, Saxons (A.D. 719–738), Swabians (A.D. 730) and Bavarians (A.D. 725–728). A diplomat as well as fighter, he sent Christian missionaries to the defeated tribes. Led by remarkable church leaders such as **St. Boniface**, the Apostle of the Germans, the missionaries converted many of the tribespeople to Christianity. Those who converted generally accepted Martel's leadership in northern and central France.

The most dramatic moment of Martel's life and career came in A.D. 732 when he responded to a request for help from **Eudes, the Duke of Aquitaine**, in southern France. Eudes found his land overrun by an invasion of Arabs from across the Pyrenees. Martel recruited a large army of Frankish warriors and led them south, seeking the Arab foe. The two armies collided at Moussais-la-Bataille, 12 miles northeast of the city of Poitiers (the battle has since been called either Poitiers or Tours).

Charles Martel at Poitiers

After seven days of maneuvering, the Arabs made their attack on the Franks. The all-day battle resulted in a standoff. The Arabs could not break the steady lines of Frankish infantry and cavalry; the Franks could not pursue the enemy quickly enough to strike a serious blow against them. Martel expected the battle to resume the next day, but daybreak found the enemy's camp deserted; the Arabs had fled during the night. Martel celebrated the victory, which has been celebrated in European history as the decisive turning point in Europe's wars against the Arabs. In the Moslem chronicles, the Battle of Poitiers figures as a small skirmish that had little overall importance.

Martel then became known as "Charles the Hammer" for this victory. He and his Frankish mounted soldiers were probably the first European military force to use stirrups on their horses. Martel died in A.D. 741, having halted Arab expansion north of Spain and having founded a new dynasty that eventually was led by his grandson **Charlemagne** (see no. 20).

20. Charlemagne

(742–814)

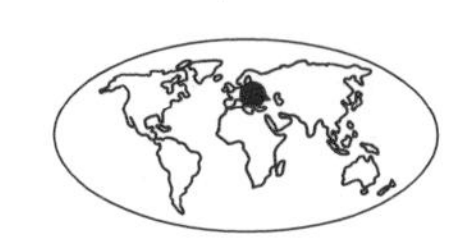

Charlemagne (SHAR-leh-main) was the greatest European warrior and king of the Middle Ages. Born in Aachen (AH-ken), in present-day Germany, he was a grandson of **Charles Martel** (see no. 19) and the son of **Pippin the Short**. Prior to his death in A.D. 768, Pippin gave the northern half of his lands to Charlemagne and the southern half to Charlemagne's brother **Carloman**.

His brother died in A.D. 771. Charlemagne seized Carloman's lands and declared himself sole king of the Franks. In A.D. 772, he responded to a call for help from Pope **Adrian I**. Charlemagne took his army into Lombardy (northeast Italy). By A.D. 774, Charlemagne was king of the Lombards as well as the Franks.

Charlemagne invaded Italy a total of five times between A.D. 772 and A.D. 778. He also invaded Moslem Spain in A.D. 778. He fought the Moslems to a draw, but on his return home, his rear guard, led by Count **Roland**, was ambushed and destroyed by Christian Basques at Roncevalles. Charlemagne's grief over the loss of Roland and his knights was later memorialized in the great epic poem "*Le Chanson de Roland*" ("The Song of Roland"), written in the 13th century.

Charlemagne

The Frankish king put down revolts in Brittany, but the greatest danger lay to the East, where the Saxon, Bavarian, and Avar tribes resisted both his rule and the Christian faith. Charlemagne fought a number of grueling battles against the Saxons, which finally ended when the Saxon leader, **Wittekind**, accepted Christianity in A.D. 785.

Charlemagne defeated the Bavarians along the Danube River in A.D. 787, but he was forced to retreat from the Avar lands in A.D. 791. A Central Asian tribe which had migrated to central Europe, the Avars had gained great wealth by extorting payments from the Byzantine emperor in Constantinople. The Frankish warriors finally defeated the Avars in A.D. 795. The wealth found in the Avar capital of Khagan made Charlemagne incredibly wealthy.

Pope **Leo III** crowned Charlemagne "King of the Romans" on Christmas Day, in A.D. 800. No European leader since the fall of the Roman Empire had controlled as much land and as many people.

Charlemagne devoted much of the last 10 years of his life to cultural enrichment. He brought **Alcuin** of York to his court at Aachen and gathered a team of other scholars who helped create the "**Carolingian Renaissance**." Books and manuscripts were copied; knowledge of Latin was renewed, and a new type of writing, known as Carolingian minuscule, came into use. The present-day use of capital and lower-case letters, punctuation and word spaces dates from the Carolingian era.

Charlemagne died in A.D. 814, leaving a troubled empire to his son, **Louis the Pious**. Tremendously successful during his lifetime, Charlemagne was unable to prevent a storm of barbarian invaders — Viking, Magyar, and Moslem — from wreaking havoc on the empire after his death. He left a rich cultural heritage and the idea of a truly united Europe.

21. Alfred the Great
(849–901)

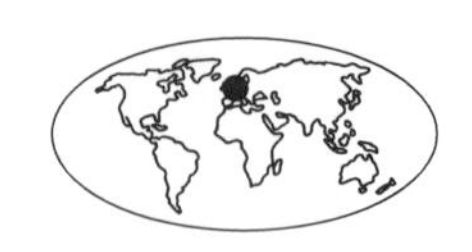

Founder of the English navy, **Alfred the Great** was born at Wantage in Berkshire, the son of King **Aethelwulft** of Wessex. The boy prince was sent to Rome at the age of four; there he met Pope **Leo IV** and was impressed by the glory of Roman Christianity. He went on a second trip to the Eternal City, this time with his father, in A.D. 855.

Alfred's father died, and his three older brothers all had short lives and reigns. To Alfred's surprise, he came to occupy the throne of Wessex at the age of 24. Alfred became king at a time of crisis for Wessex and for **Anglo-Saxon England** as a whole. Danish invaders were close to overrunning the entire land. Four Anglo-Saxon kingdoms — Mercia, Northumberland, East Anglia, and Wessex — remained, but all of them faced dire peril.

Alfred had first fought the Danes under his older brother Aethelred's leadership. In A.D. 871, the year he came to the throne, Alfred fought nine general engagements against the invaders. After losing the **Battle of Wilton**, he made an unsatisfactory peace with the Danes to give himself and his kingdom room to breathe.

Alfred the Great

Alfred married Ealhswith, a descendant of Mercian kings, and cultivated good relations with both Mercia and Wales. He built new forts in Wessex and strengthened older ones that had fallen into decay. He also built the first English ships, trying to prepare for an eventual offense against the Danes. Believing that the Danish raids were a punishment from God, he embarked on a program of religious education. He recruited important scholars from the continent and began a series of text translations from Latin into Anglo-Saxon. The king himself translated *Pastoral Care* by **Saint Gregory the Great**.

The peace ended in A.D. 876. **Guthrum**, a Danish leader, brought an army into Wessex and captured many of its important towns. Alfred himself fled to refuge in a small fort in the Somerset marshes. From there, he harassed the Danes with small raids. Alfred gathered his forces and emerged from the swamps to win a remarkable victory over the Danes at Edington in A.D. 878. Following the battle, the Danes who had surrendered were baptized as Christians. The Danes then withdrew from Wessex. Guthrum and his followers respected the peace until his death in A.D. 891.

In A.D. 892, some 250 Danish ships brought the "**Great Heathen Army**" to England. Alfred met and defeated the Danes in battle after battle. His guerrilla warfare tactics, combined with the use of his ships, allowed him to gain the upper hand quickly. By A.D. 897, the Danes had fled to East Anglia and Northumberland.

At the time of Alfred's death in A.D. 899, Wessex remained free and became the center of Anglo-Saxon law and tradition.

22. Otto the Great
(912–973)

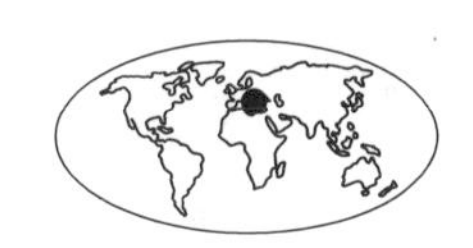

The first true imperial ruler of Germany, **Otto the Great**, was the son of King **Henry I**, known as **Henry the Fowler**. Though Henry was called "king" of Germany, he was actually first among equals of the five German dukes of Saxony, Franconia, Swabia, Bavaria and Lorraine. Otto married Edgitha, the daughter of Anglo-Saxon King **Edward the Elder** in A.D. 929. King Henry died in A.D. 936, and the dukes elected Otto to succeed his father. He was crowned at Aix-la-Chapelle, in modern-day France.

From the start, Otto was determined to turn Germany into an empire. He ruled Saxony by right of inheritance. He did away with the independent duchy of Franconia, reserving that area for himself. His most successful endeavors came through cooperation with the Christian Church. He treated the German bishops as if they were counts or dukes, giving them land and titles. In return, they owed allegiance to Otto and provided him with knights and soldiers in times of war.

Otto fought to maintain the German hold on Lorraine, an area that was disputed by the Franks to the west. He led a campaign deep into Frankish territory and brought the French kingdom of Burgundy under German influence (A.D. 940). Having secured his westward flank, Otto turned to the East and started to expand the German domains. He gained dominance over the Slavic Wends and obtained recognition of German sovereignty in Bohemia by A.D. 950.

The greatest foe of Otto's Germany was the Magyar tribe. Located in present-day Hungary, the Magyars were a fierce warrior tribe that had migrated from Central Asia around A.D. 895. The Magyars attacked Germany, France, present-day Switzerland, and Italy in numerous raids. In A.D. 955, Otto met the Magyars in battle at Lechfeld, near Augsburg, and utterly defeated them.

Otto the Great

This victory earned him the title "Otto the Great" and ended the raids from the East.

Triumphant in central Europe, Otto turned his attention southward. He cultivated good relations with the papacy, and on February 2, A.D. 962, Pope **John XII** crowned him **Holy Roman Emperor**, a title that had previously gone to the descendants of **Charlemagne** (see no. 20). Pope John turned against Otto when he saw that the German ruler wanted Italian lands. Otto used his influence in Italy to have the pope deposed and went so far as to nominate his own candidate, who became Pope **Leo VIII**.

Though he was secure in his lifetime, Otto's ambitions led to great troubles for his successors, who would fight both in Germany and Italy to hold their positions. Having formed a united German empire, Otto died in May A.D. 973 and was buried in Magdeburg Cathedral.

23. Brian Boru
(c. 941–1014)

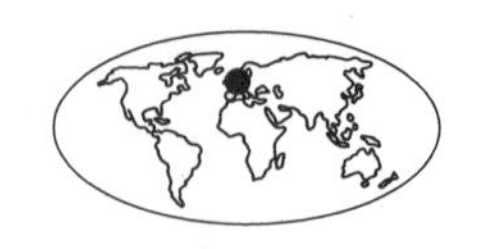

Brian Boru was born near Killaloe, in present-day County Clare, Ireland. He came from the family of **Dal Cais**, which ruled over a small principality of the same name. His father died in A.D. 951, and Brian and his older brother **Mathgamain** began a struggle against the Danes who held Limerick. For a time, Brian and only 15 men were completely on their own, living as guerrilla warriors with no home base. However, the brothers gathered their forces and defeated the Danes at the **Battle of Sulcot** (A.D. 967). Mathgamain became king of Munster.

Danish Warriors

Brian was catapulted to greater responsibility when his brother was seized and murdered in A.D. 976. Brian defeated the Danes at the **Battle of Belach Lechta** and defeated the men of Desmond. Crowned king of Munster, Brian was in a position to challenge the high king, **Mael Sechnaill II**.

During the next decade, the two kings sent raids against each others' lands. Brian had 300 boats built on the River Shannon (A.D. 984). He and his men sailed up to Loch Ree and ravaged much of the territory of Meath. Each side attacked the other many times, and in A.D. 997, Brian and the high king agreed to meet on the shore of Loch Ree. They divided Ireland between them, with Brian assuming control of the southern half of the island.

Both the Danes and many native Irish resisted his rule. Brian routed the Danes of Dublin and the Leinstermen at the **Battle of Glen Mama** (A.D. 999). As the new millennium approached, he saw his chance to become truly the "high king." In 1002, he replaced Mael Sechnaill as high king, ending a family dynasty that had endured for 200 years.

Brian consciously sought to imitate the kingly ways of **Alfred the Great** (see no. 21) and **Otto the Great** (see no. 22). He made a progression through the island and subdued Ulster in 1005. Brian's very success brought more foes against him; the Irish were unused to having a king who truly exercised the prerogatives of his title. The men of Leinster and Dublin revolted against him in 1014; they received promises of assistance from the Danes on the Isle of Man and the Orkney Islands.

One of the greatest battles in Ireland's history was fought on Good Friday, April 23, 1014. Brian, who was 73 years old, remained in his tent, praying, while his soldiers fought the **Battle of Clontarf** outside of Dublin. His son, **Murchad**, led the Irish in the battle. Brian's troops won the day, killing some 6,000 of the Leinstermen and their allies, but Brian was himself killed in the last moments of the battle by **Brodir**, chief of the Manx Vikings. Brian's son was also killed, so the Irish victory led to further confusion of leadership.

24. Canute II
(?–1035)

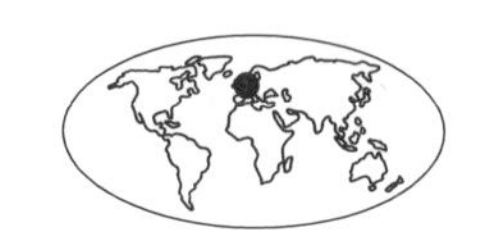

Who was this remarkable man? **Canute** was from Denmark. His father was **Sweyn Haroldson**, king of Denmark. During a campaign against Anglo-Saxon England, Sweyn died, and the Danish sailors acclaimed Canute as their new king, even though he had an older brother back in the home country. Finding he could not defeat the Anglo-Saxons, Canute returned to Denmark and gathered his forces. He returned to England in 1015 and made war on the Anglo-Saxon ruler, **Ethelred the Unready**.

Ethelred died in 1016, and was replaced by his son, **Edmund II Ironside.** The Danes won the **Battle of Ashingdon** in October and regained the "Danelaw" (northeast England) by the end of the year. Seeing the futility of war, King Edmund struck a bargain with Canute, the **Compact of Olney**. Canute received Mercia, London and Northumbria, while Edmund kept Wessex. Edmund died just weeks later, and by 1017, Canute had been acclaimed king of all England. He was the first ruler since the fall of Rome to accomplish this.

Canute came fully into power when his older brother Harold died in 1019. Now Canute was king of Denmark and England. To consolidate his gains, he married Elfgifu, the widow of King Ethelred, in 1017. He also maintained a consort of the same name, Elfgifu of Northampton.

The death of King **Olaf II** of Norway opened the way for Canute to expand even further. He fought against the Norwegians and placed that country under the rule of his mistress Elfgifu and their son Sweyn. Canute maintained control of England, Denmark and Norway, making him one of the most powerful monarchs of his day.

Canute sought to build alliances. He married his sister, Estrith, to Robert I, the duke of Normandy. He went to Rome on a pilgrimage in 1027 to improve his relations with the papacy. Canute won the trust of many of his English subjects by sending the main body of his army home to Denmark; he kept only 3,000 "**housecarls**," or bodyguards. Through warfare, diplomacy and tact, he had gained a widespread empire that ranged over thousands of miles. His fame and reputation spread.

Canute died of illness at Shaftesbury, England in 1035. His empire did not long survive him, but he had shown how a military leader could gain the respect — and perhaps even love — of his subjects.

Canute II

25. Robert Guiscard & Sichelgaita
(c. 1015–1085) & (?–1090)

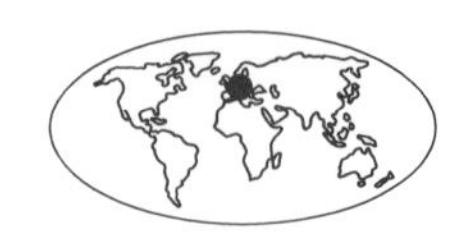

This warrior couple led their soldiers on some of the most daring raids and battles of the early Middle Ages. Born in Normandy, **Robert** (known as **Guiscard** which means "astute") was the son of **Tancred de Hauteville**, a minor noble. Guiscard came of age at a time when the Norman warriors (only three generations removed from their Viking ancestors) were the fiercest in Europe. While **William the Conqueror** led the Norman conquest of England (see no. 26), Guiscard carried out invasions in Italy and the central Mediterranean.

Guiscard was first married to Alberada of Buonalbergo, but he had the marriage annulled so he could marry **Sichelgaita**, a Lombard princess, in 1058. Like the Normans, the Lombards were a warrior people and Sichelgaita was foremost among them. She was a towering woman, imposing, muscular, and extremely courageous. She and Guiscard became true warrior partners.

Pope Gregory VII

Guiscard met Pope **Nicholas II** at Melfi, Italy, in 1059. Guiscard bowed to the pope's authority and swore to protect papal interests. Pope Nicholas invested him with the lands of southern Italy and urged him to root out the Byzantines, who held important towns there. Guiscard and Sichelgaita took 10 years to push their way down to the bottom of Italy; they expelled the last Byzantines from Bari in 1071. That was not the end of their ambitions, though. They also paved the way for a Norman invasion of Muslim Sicily, which would be carried out by Guiscard's brother, **Roger the Great**.

Guiscard and Sichelgaita threatened the papal fiefdom of Benevento in 1074; in return, they were excommunicated by the pope. The couple regained favor when Pope **Gregory VII** decided he needed their assistance to fight against Emperor **Henry IV** of the **Holy Roman Empire**.

Guiscard, Sichelgaita and **Bohemund** (Guiscard's son by his first marriage) crossed the Adriatic Sea to attack the Byzantine possessions in western Greece. They captured the cities of Corfu and Durazzo. Sichelgaita played an important role in the latter battle. Seeing some of the Normans fleeing, she galloped after them and shouted, "How far will you flee! Stand, and quit you like men!" Shamed by her words, the Normans turned, fought and won the battle.

Guiscard returned to Italy and rescued Pope Gregory from a siege conducted by the troops of Emperor Henry IV. Guiscard went back to Greece and was ready to expand his conquests when he succumbed to an epidemic at Cephalonia on July 17, 1085. Sichelgaita was with him at his death. The warrior princess played an important political role for the remaining five years of her life.

26. William the Conqueror
(c. 1027–1087)

The man who changed the history of England was born in Falaise, Normandy. **William the Conqueror** was the son of Duke **Robert** of Normandy. Though born out of wedlock, William became duke of Normandy in 1035 upon the death of his father. He was placed in the care of guardians for the next 12 years and was not able to assert his powers until 1047, when King **Henry I** of France defeated rebellious vassals of William within Normandy.

William cast an eager eye across the English Channel to Anglo-Saxon England, a country that had fallen into confusion after the death of King **Canute** (see no. 24). King **Edward the Confessor** admired the Normans, and he promised the kingdom to William upon his death, although the two men were only cousins by marriage. Edward died in 1066, and the Anglo-Saxon "**witan**" (high council) gave the throne to **Harold Godwinsson,** who was more closely related to the king than William.

William the Conqueror

Furious over this rejection, William collected an army of Norman knights at the channel and waited for the right winds to cross to England. He landed at Pevensey, England with 7,000 soldiers. William was fortunate that Harold was diverted to the north to fight an invasion of Danes. After defeating the Danes at the **Battle of Stamford Bridge,** Harold marched south to confront William. The two armies collided at Hastings.

After an exhausting contest, William's combination of cavalry and foot soldiers won the day. Harold was killed by an arrow. Following the victory, William marched to Dover, then led his men on a destructive march to London. As his troops destroyed homes and ransacked villages, the remaining Anglo-Saxon resistance began to fade. William was crowned King of England on Christmas Day, 1066.

Though the battle and crown were won, the **Norman Conquest** was not yet complete. William had to work for five years to subdue England. The resistance was strongest in the north; therefore, he led a systematic ravaging of that area in 1069–1070. By 1072, he was indeed master of England.

The third and final phase of William's career involved holding on to the vast areas he controlled. New rulers of France and Anjou challenged his rights, and he suffered setbacks at Dol (1076) and Gerberoi (1079) on the Norman border with France. He managed to keep what he had acquired. At the time of his death, William ruled over Normandy and England, a vast area that would later be the focus of much dissension between the monarchy in France and the kings of England.

21. "El Cid" (Rodrigo Diaz de Vivar) (c. 1043–1099)

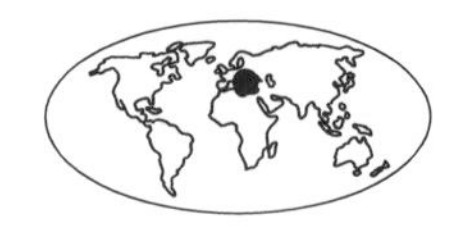

The greatest hero of the **Spanish *Reconquista*** was born in Vivar, a small town near Burgos. Son of a minor landowner, **Rodrigo Diaz de Vivar** grew up in the court of King **Ferdinand I** of the Christian kingdom of Castile. Spain was divided between several Christian kingdoms and the Moorish (Spanish Moslem) caliphate of Cordoba. The Moors had invaded Spain in A.D. 711 under the leadership of **Tariq ibn Ziyad** (see no. 17), and a religious war between the Moslems and Christians had flared in Spain ever since

Diaz grew up as a ward of Sancho, the eldest son of King Ferdinand. Upon Ferdinand's death in 1065, his territories were divided among his three sons: Sancho received Castile, Alfonso took Leon, and Garcia received Galicia. Serving under Sancho, Diaz became the foremost knight in Castile; he was now called "**El Cid**" (ell-SID; ***sidi*** is Arabic for lord).

El Cid

Sancho and El Cid expanded their holdings on the eastern section of Castile and then turned against the two younger brothers. By 1071 they had defeated Garcia, and Alfonso had been exiled. Their triumph was short-lived. Sancho was assassinated during the siege of Moslem Zamora, and Alfonso returned from exile to claim the thrones of Leon and Castile as **Alfonso VI**. El Cid had no choice but to become a leading knight in the forces of his former enemy.

For the next nine years, El Cid remained at court, surrounded by knights who had been his former foes. In 1081, he angered the king by capturing Garcia Ordonez, one of Alfonso's favorites. King Alfonso banished El Cid from the kingdom of Castile.

El Cid's life for the next nine years resembled that of Robin Hood. Leading a band of perhaps 300 men, he was an outlaw, living in the contested borderlands between the Christian kingdoms and Moslem areas. He offered his services to two Christian princes. After being rejected, he went to the Moslem city of Saragossa and led its forces for two years.

An invasion of Moslem Spain by the new **Almoravid** dynasty in 1086 led King Alfonso to reconcile with El Cid. The Moslem city of Valencia revolted against its ruler, al-Kadir, and killed him in 1092. The inhabitants awaited a takeover by a new Moslem leadership, the Almoravids, but El Cid immediately placed the city under siege with his private army. His 20-month siege ended on June 17, 1094, when the starving inhabitants surrendered.

El Cid governed Valencia for the rest of his life. He allowed freedom of worship and confirmed city dwellers in their property ownership, subject to tribute payments. He turned the great mosque of the city into a Christian church. He repulsed the Almoravid invaders outside on the plain of Cuarte, three miles west of the city in October 1094, and defeated them again at the **Battle of Bairen** in 1097.

The "*Cantar de mio Cid,*" one of the great epic poems of the Middle Ages, was written approximately 50 years after El Cid's death.

28. Saladin
(1137–1193)

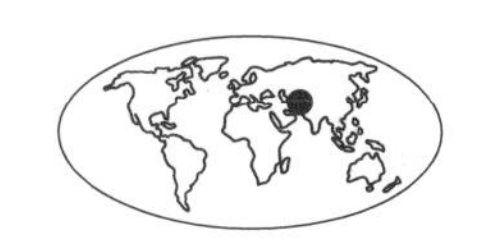

The greatest military hero of the Arab world, **Saladin** was a Kurd, born in Tikrit, Mesopotamia (present-day Iraq). He came from a prominent family; his father and uncle were advisers and soldiers of **Nur ad-Din**, who led the armies of the Moslem caliphate of Baghdad. Saladin, whose name in Arabic means "the bounty of religion," interrupted his theological studies to join his uncle, Shirkuh, on a campaign against Egypt. That country was ruled by the **Fatmid** caliphate, which orthodox Moslems such as Saladin considered heretical.

Saladin led a heroic defense of the city of Alexandria, Egypt, against a joint force of Egyptians and Christian crusaders in 1167. His uncle died in 1169, and Saladin was immediately named commander of the Syrian troops in Egypt. He finished the work his uncle had begun by ending the Fatmid caliphate and establishing himself as the Moslem leader of Egypt. Grateful for his work in eliminating the Fatmid heresy, the Abbasid caliph in Damascus approved his new position.

Nur ad-Din died in 1174, and Saladin stretched himself and his resources in order to take over Syria. By 1176, he was sultan of both Egypt and Syria and was able to contemplate an attack on the Christian-held land that lay between his two domains: Palestine, which the Christians had conquered during the **First Crusade** (1095–1099).

Saladin called for a ***jihad*** (holy war) against the Christians in 1187. He gathered an army of 12,000 cavalry, attended by as many retainers and foot soldiers. Maneuvering with skill, Saladin lured his Christian foes out of the safety of the city of Jerusalem and onto an arid stretch of land by the Sea of Galilee. The **Battle of the Horns of Hattin** (two large hills by the water) was fought on July 4, 1187. Saladin won a complete victory. He treated King **Guy** of Jerusalem with dignity but had all the **Christian Knights Templar** executed. Saladin pressed home his advantage and entered Jerusalem in triumph.

Acting with unusual benevolence, Saladin allowed the Christian population to ransom itself with payments of gold. His triumph was incomplete, however, because three Christian cities on the shore of the Mediterranean — Antioch, Tripoli and Tyre — held out against him. Christian Europe rallied to oppose the new Arab takeover of the Holy Land, and in 1191, King **Richard** of England (see no. 29) and King **Philip Augustus** of France arrived at Acre to fight Saladin.

Saladin could not overcome the battle skills of "Richard the Lion-Hearted." The English king was unable to capture Jerusalem, though. Therefore, the two kings agreed to a three-year truce (signed September 2, 1192) that left Jerusalem in Arab hands but guaranteed Christian pilgrims the right to visit the city.

Worn out from his battles and campaigns, Saladin went to Damascus for a rest. He died there of a fever. His greatest accomplishment was his unification of the Arab world in the face of the Crusader threat.

Horns of Hattin

29. Richard the Lion-Hearted
(1157–1199)

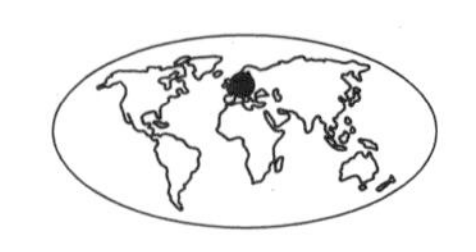

The greatest Christian warrior of the Middle Ages was born in 1157, the third child of King **Henry II** of England and Queen **Eleanor** of **Aquitaine** (southeast France). **Richard** grew up in a stormy household environment that has been vividly recreated in the movie *The Lion in Winter* (released in 1968). From an early age, Richard was the favorite child of his mother, but he also fought with his father on numerous occasions.

As duke of Aquitaine, Richard revolted against his father in 1173–1174 and again in 1188–1189. He was close to success on the second occasion when his father died, leaving Richard king of England as well as duke of Aquitaine and Normandy. He was crowned in England on September 3, 1189. Though he is acclaimed as a national hero by the English, Richard was essentially a Norman knight, and he spoke French far more readily than English.

Richard the Lion-Hearted

A true warrior-king, in 1187, Richard heeded the call of the **Third Crusade**, a war intended to recapture Jerusalem from the Arab leader **Saladin** (see no. 28). Richard allied with other Christian rulers, including King **Philip Augustus** of France and Emperor **Frederick Barbarossa** ("Frederick the Red Beard") of Germany. The three kings planned the joint crusade together. Philip and Richard sailed to the Holy Land while Barbarossa marched overland. Barbarossa drowned in a stream in Asia Minor (present-day Turkey), and most of his army turned back.

After the Christians captured Acre in the Holy Land, Richard ordered the slaughter of 2,600 prisoners, whom he could not afford to feed. Philip Augustus pled illness and returned to France, where he immediately began to chip away at Richard's lands in Aquitaine and Normandy. The Christian king outfought and outmaneuvered Saladin in two important battles, but was unable to capture Jerusalem itself. Feeling pressure from Philip's incursions on his homelands, Richard signed a three-year truce with Saladin and returned home.

He made the mistake of going through Germany. He was spotted, captured and held prisoner by the duke of Austria, who was an ally of Philip Augustus. England was forced to raise 150,000 marks of silver to ransom Richard. Released in 1194, he went to England only briefly, then went to Normandy and spent the next five years fighting against Philip. Richard won nearly every battle and retook all the land and castles that had been lost in his absence. Richard was struck in the left shoulder by a crossbow arrow while trying to capture the castle of Chalus in Limoges. The wound became infected, and he died 10 days later. He had spent only six months of his 10-year reign in England itself.

30. Genghis Khan
(c. 1167–1227)

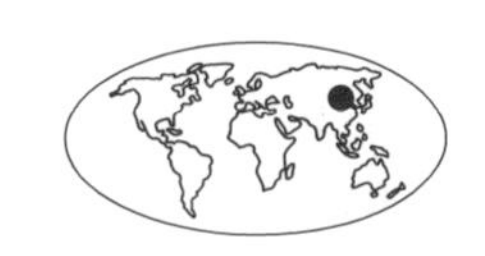

Possibly no world leader has ever inspired more fear and dread as **Temujin**, better known as **Genghis Khan**. Born near the Onon River in present-day Mongolia, Temujin was the son of **Yesugei,** chief of the Borjigin tribe of **Mongols**. His father was poisoned by **Tatar** tribespeople when Temujin was nine, and he grew up on his own in the fierce environment of the competing Mongol tribes. Early on he set a pattern of skillful leadership both in diplomacy and battle. In 1206, the ***huraltai*** (great assembly) of Mongols named him "Genghis Khan," or supreme leader.

Khan united the Tatar, Kereit, Naiman and Merkit tribes into one fearsome band of Mongol warriors. The Mongols had long been renowned as warriors, but Khan molded them into a more disciplined force that allowed them to win greater victories. He developed a system of mobile horse columns which would encircle and entrap a foe, and then kill them using armor-piercing arrows.

Khan began his campaign for world mastery by attacking the Chin Empire of northern China. The Chin people had long withstood invasions behind their **Great Wall of China**, but the Mongols outflanked the defenders and attacked the heartland of northern China. The Mongols captured the great city of **Peking** in 1215, showing that they could employ sophisticated strategies in siege warfare as well as in combat on the open plains.

Genghis Khan

Khan then turned his wrath upon the Kharismian Empire of present-day Afghanistan and Iran. After the Kharismian ruler killed Khan's envoys, the Mongols descended on their new enemy with a speed and ferocity that scarcely seemed possible. Khan besieged and captured Samarkand, the center of the empire; the sack that followed was the worst of the many conducted by the Mongols.

Khan sent his best general, **Subotai** (see no. 31), north to pursue the son of the Kharismian leader who had died. Subotai pursued, but did not catch the prince, he was, however, drawn north to Russia, where he defeated a large army led by the princes of Kiev. The result was that southern Russia would be under the "Mongol yoke" for three centuries and therefore would miss the effects of the **Renaissance** in Europe.

Khan conducted another successful campaign in northern India. He ravaged Moslem cities there before returning to Mongolia in 1224. Khan then turned his attention to China once more. He attacked the Hsi Hsia Empire, located in north-central China. As the campaign began, Khan fell from his horse while on a hunting expedition. He suffered internal injuries and a fever and died rather suddenly, at the height of his power and prestige.

Khan's Mongol warriors buried his body on a hill in the Kentei Mountains of present-day Mongolia. The hill was known as the sacred mountain of **Burdan-kaldun**; several of Genghis Khan's descendants would later be buried beside him. Trees then grew up obscuring the spot, and no one today can identify the grave of one of the world's greatest conquerors.

31. Subotai (c. 1176–1248)

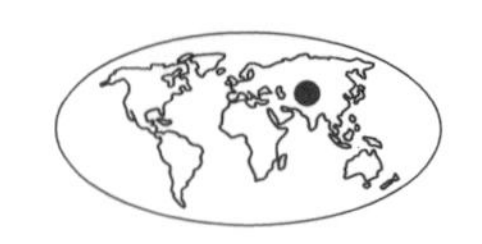

Subotai became one of **Genghis Khan**'s most trusted generals during the war against the Chin Empire (see no. 30). After Khan destroyed the Kharismian Empire in Persia, Subotai went north in pursuit of the son of the former Kharismian shah. They crushed Christian Georgia and entered the land of the Kiptchak Turks in southern Russia.

Subotai explored and ravaged the area before wintering on the Black Sea in 1223. Subotai returned to central Asia, and completed the conquest of the Chin Empire.

Battle of Liegnitz

In 1237, Subotai was made co-commander (with **Batu Khan**, grandson of Genghis Khan) of the Mongol forces in southern Russia. With Subotai acting as the military genius, and Batu representing the power and importance of the **Genghisid** line, the Mongols captured the Moscow area. In December 1240, they destroyed the Russian principality of Kiev.

In the 16 years that had passed since he had been on the Black Sea, Subotai developed an extensive network of spies in eastern Europe. His goal was to subdue the Christian kingdom of Hungary. Subotai was especially anxious to do this since the Hungarians were the only peoples of Mongol-Turkic descent who had yet to acknowledge the overlordship of the Genghisid family in central Asia.

Four "flying columns" or army groups carried out the invasion. Prince **Kaidu** led the first group northeast into Poland; he defeated the Poles and their allies at Szydlow and Liegnitz (near Kraków). With his right flank covered, Subotai plunged into Hungary with the three other columns. Following Mongol strategy to perfection, the three army groups rode by different routes, but all converged on the Danube River by April 4, 1241.

Led by King **Bela**, the Hungarian army was camped on the west bank of the river. Seeing the strength of his foe, Subotai retreated 100 miles northeast and positioned himself on the east bank of the Sajo River. Bela followed him, and on April 10, the Hungarians established a small bridgehead on the eastern bank.

Early in the morning of April 11, Bela's troops were hit by a massive Mongol attack on the bridgehead. The Mongols fought their way across and attacked the main Hungarian camp. The battle was evenly matched until Subotai came seemingly out of nowhere with 30,000 men; they had crossed the river south of the Hungarians the night before. The hard-fought battle turned into a tremendous rout. By noon, the Hungarian army was destroyed, and between 40,000–70,000 Hungarians lost their lives on the field.

In December 1241, he learned that **Ogedi Khan**, son of Genghis Khan, had died. Mindful of his duty to the Mongol law code, Subotai sent the princes he had with him home to participate in the vote that would name a new great khan. Subotai himself took leave of the Mongol court and retired to die alone in his tent on the steppes of northern Asia.

32. Kublai Khan
(1215–1294)

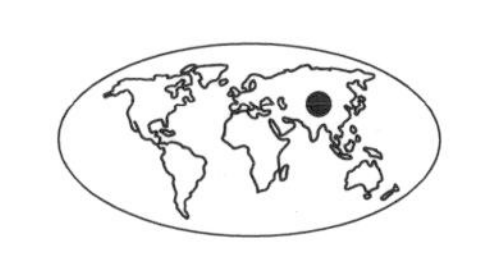

Although he is generally associated with trade, prosperity and the visit of Marco Polo, **Kublai Khan** was indeed a warrior. His mother, Sorghagtani Beki, groomed all four of her sons as prospective heirs to the **Mongol Empire**. Her husband Tolui had been passed over in the succession, and she was determined the same thing would not happen to her sons. A fervent Nestorian Christian, Beki won influence and the respect of much of the Mongol elite. She died in 1252, having had the satisfaction of seeing Mangu, Kublai's older brother, take the throne in 1251.

Kublai Khan

Kublai began his military career during the 1250s. He led an epic expedition that took control of the kingdom of Ta-li (present-day Yunnan province in southwest China) in 1252–1254. Kublai led his 100,000 troops through 1,000 miles of ice-capped mountains on the eastern border of present-day Tibet. Only 20,000 of the men survived the journey. Kublai led another army south against the Sung Empire, while his veterans in Yunnan traveled by a different route to join him. Thus, by the time Mangu Khan died in 1259, Kublai had become a seasoned military leader. He emerged as the new ***khagan***, or universal ruler in June of 1260.

Kublai Khan turned southward and concentrated his force on the Sung Empire of southern China. While the northern Chin and Hsi Hsia Empires had been peopled by mixed ethnic backgrounds, the Sung Empire was fully and truly Chinese. Kublai showed the care and thorough preparation for which he had become known as he slowly conquered China. He captured the Sung capital of Hangchow (1276), and the last Sung resistance ended in 1279. Kublai thereby reunified China for the first time since the T'ang Dynasty had fallen in the 10th century. He also ruled over 80 percent of the entire Eurasian landmass, perhaps the largest empire in all of human history.

Kublai led his troops even further south. He invaded Annam (present-day northern Vietnam) and defeated the Pagon king of Burma. In these southern invasions, the Mongols faced elephants in battle for the first time. After winning their victories, they brought many elephants north to China, where they became a fixture in Kublai's court. Kublai sent an invasion fleet to the island of Java in 1293, but the mission was defeated when his Javanese allies turned against the Mongols.

He died in 1294, having indeed brought China to unity. His body was brought to the sacred mountain in Mongolia called **Burdankaldun**, where he was laid to rest next to his grandfather, **Genghis Khan** (see no. 30).

33. Edward I
(1239–1307)

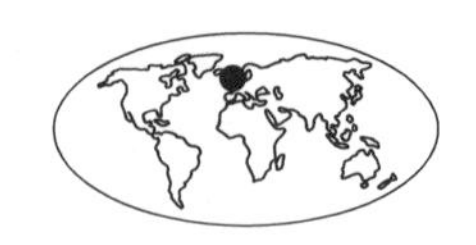

The most skillful and ruthless ruler of his age, **Edward "Longshanks"** expanded the size of England at the expense of its neighboring peoples. Born at Westminster, Edward was the son of King **Henry III** and Eleanor of Provence. He married Eleanor of Castile in 1254.

Edward's early years were plagued by the "**Baron's War**" that pitted King Henry III against the most ambitious of his lords. Edward won the culminating victory in the war in 1266. Then he followed his admired uncle, King **Louis IX** of **France**, on a crusade to North Africa. Following Louis death, Edward went to Syria, then returned to Europe. His father had died during the crusade; Edward put down a revolt in Aquitaine and made his way to London where he was crowned in 1274.

The Parliament of Edward I

Edward faced an immediate challenge in the person of **Llewelyn ap Gruffudd**, the leading prince of **Wales**, who refused to acknowledge the English king as his overlord. Edward waged a series of fierce campaigns in the **Welsh Wars** (1277–1284), which ended with the death of Gruffudd and the execution of his brother. Edward incorporated Wales fully into the kingdom, bringing English common law to Wales. In 1301, his son became the first **Prince of Wales**, and this is still the title traditionally held by the heir apparent to the British throne.

France and Scotland posed even greater threats to Edward's status as the great king of his day. A succession crisis in Scotland, following the death of King **Alexander III**, played into Edward's hands. He declared his preference for **John de Baliol** in the struggle for the Scottish throne. In 1296, Edward invaded Scotland, defeated the assembled clans, and brought the **Stone of Scone**, the symbol of Scottish power, to England. (It sits today in London's Westminster Abbey.)

Sir **William Wallace** (commemorated in the 1995 movie, *Braveheart*) resisted Edward's attempts to rule Scotland indirectly. Edward marched north in 1298. Through skillful use of archers and cavalrymen, he completely vanquished Wallace's army at the **Battle of Falkirk**. Remarkably, the Scottish independence movement did not collapse. Even the capture and execution of Wallace in 1305 did not bring Scotland to heel.

Edward marched to Scotland one more time. He died near Carlisle, leaving a much expanded kingdom to his son, **Edward III**. He had inaugurated some crucial English traditions that remain important today: the status of the Prince of Wales, the calling of **Parliament** to raise funds, and the sovereignty of England over Wales and Scotland.

34. Robert Bruce
(1274–1329)

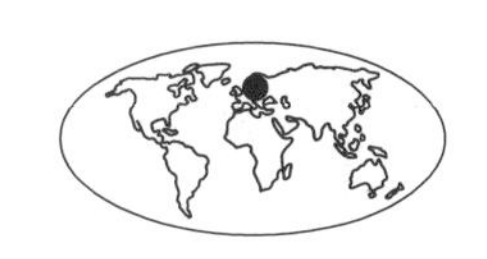

A tenacious and resourceful fighter, **Robert the Bruce** braved many dark hours to free Scotland from English rule. Probably born in Turnberry Castle in Scotland, he was the son of **Robert de Bruce VII**, the earl of Carrick. Robert the Bruce followed his father's lead in foreign policy for many years. Both the Bruces paid homage to English King **Edward I** (see no. 33) in 1296. Robert Bruce actually took up arms to serve with Edward at the **Battle of Falkirk**, where England crushed the Scottish freedom fighters led by Sir **William Wallace**.

Until his father's death in 1304, Robert Bruce sought to exercise some type of rule in Scotland under the dominion of King Edward I. After 1305, Robert collected his forces and planned a master stroke against the English. Seeing what happened to Wallace, who was drawn and quartered, Robert still took the leadership of the Scottish independence movement. In April 1306, he quarreled with and murdered **John Comyn**, a competitor for the throne, at a church in Dumfries. Robert was crowned King of Scotland at Scone on March 27, 1306.

His first efforts were failures. He was defeated at the **Battle of Methven** on June 19, 1306, and became a fugitive. Only the death of Edward I in 1307 brought some hope to Robert's cause. An old Scottish legend has it that during this time, Robert watched a spider try seven times to connect a web. Seeing the spider finally succeed, Robert resolved that he too would continue the fight.

After 1307, the Bruce led a slow and concerted effort to capture the English fortresses and castles within Scotland. He took Dundee and Perth (1312–1313) and Edinburgh and Roxburgh (1314) and was close to success when **Edward II** approached with an English army three times the size of the Scottish forces. On June 24, 1314, Robert's inspired leadership and the sheer determination of the Scottish "**schiltrons**" (groups of pikemen) won the **Battle of Bannockburn**. Edward II was routed and nearly captured. Robert carried the war to northern England.

In 1323, the pope recognized Robert the Bruce's title as king of Scotland. Robert successfully resisted another English invasion in 1322, and in 1327, he purposefully broke another truce. His military success gave the English no choice — they recognized his title and Scotland's independence in the **Treaty of Northampton**, signed in March 1328.

Robert had only one year in which to enjoy his victory. He died in 1329 of a wasting disease that may have been leprosy. He was the subject of a romantic poem, "The Bruce," written by John Barbour in the 1370s.

Robert the Bruce and William Wallace

35. Edward the Black Prince
(1330–1376)

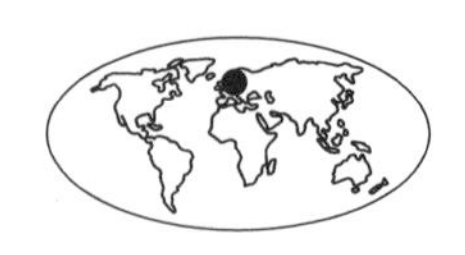

Capture of John II at Poitiers

Known as the "**Black Prince**" because of the color of his armor, **Edward** was the oldest son of King **Edward III** and Philippa of Hainault. Born at the royal manor of Woodstock in Oxfordshire, he became **Prince of Wales** in 1343 and was schooled in both diplomacy and war.

At the early age of 16, Edward led the vanguard of the English army at the **Battle of Crecy** (1346). The crushing English victory was partly attributed to his leadership. The blind king of Bohemia, who fought and died with the French that day, earned Edward's admiration, and he took for himself the king's motto, "***ich dien,***" or "I serve." It remains the motto of the Prince of Wales to this day.

In 1355, Edward was given command of the English troops in Aquitaine (southern France). He led them in a resounding victory over the French at the **Battle of Poitiers**. King **John the Good** of France was taken prisoner, as were 2,000 other Frenchmen. The English victory was attributed to Edward's skill and daring.

He married Joan, the countess of Kent, in 1361. The royal couple moved to France together and stayed there for eight years. Edward showed himself to be a poor administrator; he alienated the local nobles and infuriated them with high taxes. In 1367, he led an invasion across the Pyrenees Mountains into Spain, and he defeated the Spanish at the **Battle of Najera**, near Burgos. Still, the increased expenses led to further taxes, which enraged his subjects in Aquitaine even more.

Edward put down a major rebellion of his subjects by sacking Limoges in 1370. Around this time he was summoned by the King of France to appear in Paris and explain his conduct. Edward's reply was that he would appear, helmeted and with 60,000 men. This statement was a bluff, for the Prince was slowly dying from dysentery and dropsy he had acquired during the Spanish campaign. Following the death of his oldest son, he resigned his position and went to Berkhampstead, England to live his last years as a semi-invalid. He made one major appearance before the English **Parliament** (1376) to ensure that the throne would pass to his second-oldest son. Edward died in 1376, one year before his father.

Known as the most chivalrous knight in Europe, Edward evoked great fear among his foes. He never lost a battle. His shield and armor were hung above his tomb at Canterbury, replicas of which tourists can see today.

36. Tamerlane
(1336–1405)

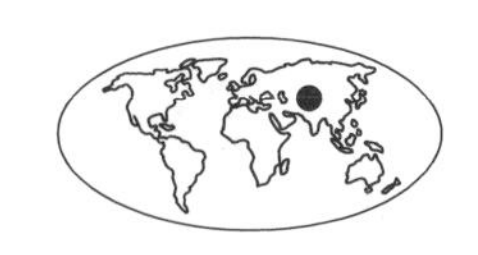

The great conqueror of central Asia was born near Kesh, in present-day Uzbekistan. He was of a tribe that had a mixed Turkish and Mongol heritage, the Barulas. Wounded by an arrow in his early life, he was called "**Timur-i Lang**," meaning "Timur the Lame," which westerners changed over time to **Tamerlane**.

Tamerlane grew up hearing tales of the glorious conquests of **Genghis Khan** (see no. 30) in the golden city of Samarkand. Intensely ambitious, he defeated all his local rivals to become the regional governor of Transoxiana, of which Samarkand was the capital. Still, he needed to establish himself as a worthy successor to Khan. Therefore, he married Saray Mulk Khanum, a princess of the Genghisid line. Though she bore him no children, she remained his chief wife throughout his life.

Once he felt secure in his home province, Tamerlane turned southwest and made war against the kingdom of Khurasan (1381) in present-day Iran. He penetrated even further west and reached occupied Sistan.

Around the age of 40, Tamerlane commenced a series of spectacular campaigns which established him as the greatest conqueror of his day. He made savage attacks on Christian Armenia and Georgia in the late 1380s. Then, he was caught by surprise when **Tokhtamish** (a former protégé and leader of the Golden Horde in southern Russia) made war against him. Tamerlane went north with an army of 200,000 men. His Mongol foes withdrew for hundreds of miles before finally giving battle at the confluence of the Kama and Volga rivers. Tamerlane won an overwhelming victory. In revenge for Tokhtamish's disloyalty, he changed the trade routes so that caravans went south of the Caspian Sea and through his territory.

During the **Five Years' Campaign** (1392–1397), Tamerlane terrorized virtually all his neighbors in central Asia. He then turned south and attacked the Delhi sultanate in northern India. He captured Delhi and conducted an enormous massacre of prisoners.

Once again, his interest and direction shifted. Tamerlane attacked the Christian states in the Middle East and was drawn into a tremendous confrontation with **Bayezid**, leader of the Ottoman Turks. After exchanging insults by messenger, the two leaders clashed at the **Battle of Angora** (1402). Tamerlane won and kept Bayezid as a personal prisoner until his death.

In 1404, Tamerlane laid out comprehensive plans for a campaign against China. He set out from Samarkand late in the year with an enormous army. His health finally gave out and he died at Otrar in present-day Kazahkstan.

The greatest military leader of his century, Tamerlane was the last of the great conquerors from the steppes, the great plains of southeast Europe and Asia.

Tamerlane

37. Bayezid I (1354–1403)

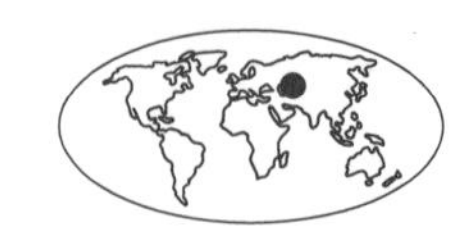

Nicknamed "**The Thunderbolt**" for the lightning speed of his maneuvers, **Bayezid** was the son of Sultan **Murad I** of the Ottoman Empire. Bayezid began his career as governor of Anatolia (part of Turkey) and gained the throne in 1389 upon the death of his father.

In the 40 years prior to Bayezid's ascension to the throne, the **Ottoman Turks** had crossed the Sea of Marmara and acquired large sections of land in eastern Europe, though they had not conquered Constantinople. Bayezid first dealt with revolts in both Anatolia and the Balkans. The remarkable swiftness with which he moved across the Sea of Marmara to direct these operations earned him his nickname.

Bayezid waged a war of extermination in Thrace (the European section of the Byzantine Empire). He was called to Anatolia in 1394, where he put down more revolts against his rule. His blockade of Constantinople led Byzantine Emperor **Manuel II** to plead for help from Christian Europe. Pope **Boniface IX** called for a crusade and King **Sigismund** of Hungary and the dukes of the French provinces of Burgundy and Nevers led an army of between 50,000–100,000 men to eastern Europe.

Bayezid met the crusader force at Nicopolis on September 28, 1396. He routed the European army and ended any chance for western Europe to relieve the pressure on Constantinople. From that time forward, the Ottoman possession of the Balkans region was secure.

Following his victory at Nicopolis, Bayezid concentrated on reducing Constantinople. He continued the blockade and seemed nearly ready to launch an all-out assault when he was summoned in a letter from **Tamerlane** (see no. 36). Tamerlane was irritated by Bayezid's actions in eastern Turkey and Syria. He commanded Bayezid to return all land he had taken from the Byzantines. The irony of one Moslem Turk commanding another to be good to the Orthodox Christian Byzantines was not lost on Bayezid. He refused the summons and sent back an insolent reply, which led to an all-out confrontation between the two greatest Turkish leaders of the day.

Bayezid I captured at Angora

Bayezid marched into eastern Anatolia; Tamerlane marched east and met him at Angora. The two armies maneuvered for some time before Tamerlane forced Bayezid into battle by cutting off the Ottomans from their water supply. The battle was hard-fought, but Tamerlane prevailed and Bayezid was brought as a prisoner before him. Tamerlane treated his prisoner as a slave, and Bayezid is reputed to have undergone numerous humiliations prior to his death in Baghdad one year later.

38. Jan Ziska
(c. 1358–1424)

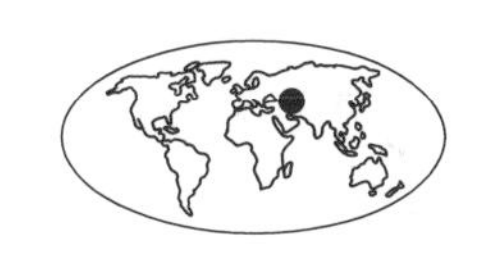

Known as "**The One-Eyed,**" **Jan Ziska** led the **Hussites** in a religious and patriotic war against the Holy Roman Empire. Born in Trocnov, Bohemia (present-day Czechoslovakia), Ziska lost an eye in childhood. He served in the military bands of several Bohemian lords and went to Poland to fight against the **Teutonic Knights**, an order of German knights. He particularly distinguished himself at the **Battle of Tannenberg** in 1410. He became an adherent of the church reforms advocated by **Jan Hus**, which many scholars see as the start of the **Protestant Reformation**.

Following the death of Bohemian King **Wenceslas IV** in 1419, his half brother Emperor **Sigismund** of the **Holy Roman Empire** claimed the throne of Bohemia. Sigismund announced his intention to root out all heresy from his new kingdom. Learning of the emperor's plan, Ziska formed a band of 400 men who called themselves the "**armed brotherhood of Taborites**" (Tabor was a city in south-central Bohemia). The Taborites occupied the Vitkov heights over the city of Prague. When Sigismund's troops arrived in 1420, they saw Ziska's defenses and withdrew from the area without trying to capture the city. (Since that time the heights have been called Zizkov in his honor.)

Ziska developed a fighting system that was completely new. He mounted cannons on farm wagons, which could be drawn together at a moment's notice to form a prodigious defense. The Hussite battle plan almost always called for a resolute defense from the wagons, followed at a crucial moment by an attack from behind the wagons that would rout the enemy. Ziska also pioneered in the development of earthwork fortifications.

Using these new tactics, Ziska defeated the emperor's soldiers at Plzen (1421), Kutna Hora and Nemecky Brod (1422). He himself lost his remaining sight at the siege of the castle at Rabi, but continued to direct his troops. In 1423, there was a serious breach between the radical Taborites and a more moderate Bohemian group called the Utraquists. A Hussite civil war ensued in which Ziska led the Taborites to victory at Horid and Strachor.

Ziska took command of another sect of radical Hussites in eastern Bohemia based around the mountain fort of Hradec Kraloue (better known as Horeb). He continued to win victories over the moderate Hussite elements, notably at Malesov on June 7, 1424.

Ziska contracted the bubonic plague and died at the castle of Pribyslav. He was buried at Horeb, but his remains were later transferred to Caslav. Ziska remains one of the national heroes of Bohemia, a land that has known many conquerors since his time period.

Jan Ziska

39. Joan of Arc
(c. 1412–1431)

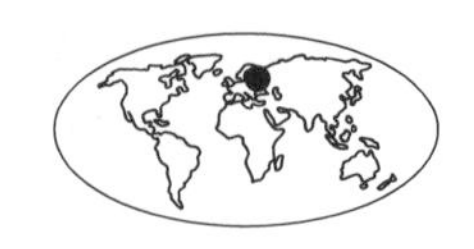

Joan of Arc at Orleans

A peasant girl who became a warrior and saved a monarchy, **Joan of Arc** was born in the village of Domremy in northeast France. Joan grew up amidst the turmoil of the **Hundred Years' War** between France and England. England's King **Henry V** had smashed the French army at Agincourt in 1415 and set his son up as the new king in Paris. **Charles VII** of France, the uncrowned *dauphin* (doe-FAN) (crown prince) fled to the Loire River valley.

Around the age of 13, Joan began to have religious visions and hear voices. She claimed that saints Michael, Margaret and Catherine came to her and told her that she was destined to save France from the English. As she grew older, the visions increased in intensity, and at the age of 17, she presented herself to the local fort commander and asked for safe passage to see the dauphin. She was turned away twice but on her third request, **Robert de Baudricourt** gave her a horse and an escort of armed men. Traveling by night, with muffled hooves, the party evaded the English scouts and reached the dauphin's court at Chinon on the Loire.

Charles VII was naturally surprised that a peasant girl should ride a horse, much less tell him she intended to save his throne. The dauphin turned her over to a group of religious scholars. They examined Joan and proclaimed she was of sound mind and not delusional.

The great crisis hanging over France was the English siege of the key city of **Orleans**. Further resistance seemed hopeless if Orleans fell. The dauphin gave command of 4,000 men to Joan and bade her do her best.

Arriving at Orleans at the end of April, she directed the French movements in an inspired counterattack that forced the English to lift the siege. She pushed northward, invading territory held by the English for nearly 10 years. She led the French cavalry in an attack that won the **Battle of Patay**, the first major defeat for the English in many years. Joined by the dauphin, Joan pressed on to **Rheims Cathedral**, where on July 17, 1429, the dauphin, Charles, was anointed and crowned King Charles VII. In less than three months, she had won major victories and ensured the survival of the **Valois** monarchy.

On May 23, 1430, Joan was captured by Burgundian soldiers (Frenchmen allied with the English). She was sold to the English for 16,000 francs and brought to the city of **Rouen**, where she was tried for heresy. The trial was an ecclesiastical (church) trial, but the English had engineered matters so she would be found guilty of wearing men's clothing and claiming she heard the voices of saints. Joan was convicted, sentenced and burned at the stake at Rouen on May 30, 1431.

A court trial in 1456 found that Joan had been sentenced improperly. She was canonized (made a saint) in 1920.

40. Mehmed II, the Conqueror
(1432–1481)

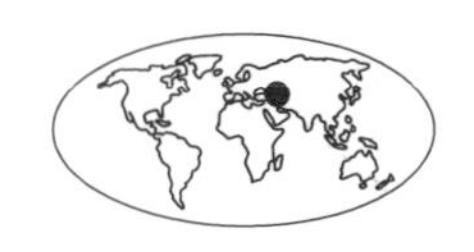

The Ottoman leader who captured Constantinople was born in Edirne, Turkey. **Mehmed** was the son of **Murad II**, sultan of the **Ottoman Empire**. His father gave him the Ottoman throne in 1444 in order to avoid the customary succession struggles. Internal political problems forced Murad II to take the leadership back from 1446 until 1451. Upon his death in 1451, Mehmed II became sultan.

Mehmed faced opposition from both his grand vizier, **Halil Pasha Candarli**, and a "peace party" within the empire. He felt that the only way to guarantee his position as sultan was to capture **Constantinople**, the capital of the **Byzantine Empire**.

Mehmed brought an enormous Ottoman army to the walls of Constantinople in the spring of 1453. He brought forth huge cannons; the largest required 50 teams of oxen to pull and 200 men to hold it in balance. The Ottoman artillery knocked down large sections of the walls that had withstood so many would-be conquerors in the past. On May 29, the Ottomans entered the city, killed the last Byzantine emperor, and ended 1300 years of Christian rule. Mehmed entered the city later that day. Greatly impressed with the architecture of the **Hagia Sophia**, the city's beautiful church, he renamed it **Aya Sofya** (pride of the sultan) and turned it into a mosque. From that day on he was known as ***Fatih***, meaning "the Conqueror."

Mehmed expanded his empire westward, conquering Serbia (but not the city of Belgrade) in 1459. He took all of Greece, conquered Moldavia (1462), and incorporated Bosnia and Herzegovina into the Ottoman Empire. He used the Ottoman fleet to cut vital trade routes that Venetian and Genoan ships depended upon and, after a long war (1465–1479), received annual payments of tribute from Venice.

One area withstood the Ottoman conquest. Prince **Vlad III** of Walachia (known as "**Vlad the Impaler**") fended off a major assault by the Ottomans in 1462. The sight of hundreds of their fellows impaled on high stakes along a roadway persuaded even the fierce Ottoman troops to turn about.

Mehmed expanded eastward as well. He finally subdued the Karaman-oglu, a rival Turkish tribe in eastern Anatolia (Turkey). He increased the size and strength of the elite Janissary corps and made the Janissaries loyal to the sultan, rather than to the empire as a whole. Mehmed died in 1481. He left a vigorous empire built on a combination of religious fanaticism and tribal allegiances. At the peak of power he considered himself to be the ***khan*** (emperor of the Turkic nomads), ***ghazi*** (fighter for the religion of Islam), and ***basileus*** (successor to the Byzantine emperors).

Mehmed II, the Conqueror

41. Francisco Pizarro
(c. 1470–1541)

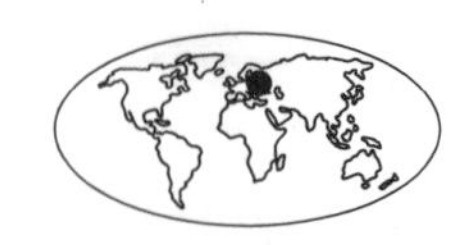

Francisco Pizarro was born in Trujillo, Estremadura, Spain. He entered the Spanish army at an early age. Shaped by leaders such as Gonzalo Fernanadez de Cordoba, the Spanish military was the most sophisticated and advanced in Europe.

Francisco Pizarro at Cajamarca

Pizarro went to Santo Domingo in the Caribbean in 1502 and served on the unsuccessful colonizing adventure of Alonso de Ojeda in 1509. He made the first crossing of Panama with the great explorer Balboa (1513) and settled there. Hearing of an Indian empire of enormous wealth, he formed a partnership with **Diego de Almagro**, a soldier, and **Hernando de Luque**, a priest. Pizarro and Almagro explored along the Pacific coast of present-day Colombia (1524–1525; 1526–1528). On their second voyage, they reached a prosperous Indian town in present-day Ecuador and returned with gold, llamas, and Indians who spoke of the wealth of the **Inca Empire**.

Pizarro went to Spain in 1528, where the **Council of the Indies** made him captain-general and governor of any lands he might conquer. The Council provided no funds, however, and Almagro resented the lesser titles he received from Spain.

Pizarro returned to Panama, and in January 1531, set out with 180 men, 27 horses and two small cannons. Traveling both by land and water, he reached the town of San Miguel de Piura, which he used as a base. In September 1532, he entered the Andes with no more than 200 men, a tiny force with which to confront the Incas.

The Inca Empire has just ended a civil war between two brothers: **Atahualpa** (at-ah-WHALP-ah) and **Huascar**. Atahualpa prevailed, only to learn of a new threat: Pizarro and his band of intrepid followers. Atahualpa allowed the Spaniards to come inland to the town of Cajamarca. There, the Spaniards lured the Inca leader into an ambush. The 200 Spaniards terrified and defeated several thousand Incas with their swords, guns, horses and dogs. The **Battle of Cajamarca** (November 16, 1532) gave Pizarro custody of Atahualpa, and therefore the leadership of the Inca Empire. Although Atahualpa raised an enormous ransom — some records say it was a huge room filled to the ceiling with gold — Pizarro had the Inca leader executed on August 19, 1533.

Pizarro founded **Lima** as the capital of his new domain. Almagro became his bitter rival. Almagro, after failing to capture Chile, returned to Peru and seized the city of Cuzco. Pizarro's brother captured and killed Almagro, whose followers were deprived of their land and estates. Bitter over their losses, his followers and friends formed a conspiracy and killed Pizarro at his palace in Lima on June 26, 1541.

42. Zahiruddin Mohammed Babar
(1483–1530)

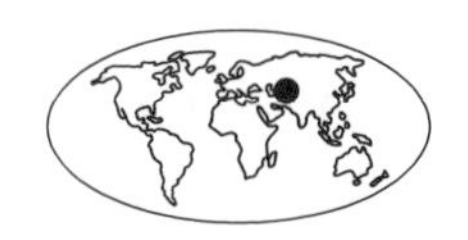

Zahiruddin Mohammed Babar, whose name means "tiger" in the Mongol tongue, was a **Chugtai Turk**, born in present-day Turkestan. On his father's side, he was a fifth-generation descendant of **Tamerlane** (see no. 36) and on his mother's side, he was 14 generations removed from **Genghis Khan** (see no. 30). Babar was the son of **Omar Shaikh**, who ruled the small central Asian principality of Fergana.

Babar inherited the throne from his father at the age of 12. He wanted to conquer and hold the city of Samarkand, which had been the city of Tamerlane and the Timurid dynasty. Seeking to fulfill that goal, Babar fought relentlessly, and futilely, against **Shaibani Khan**, leader of the **Uzbek Turks**. Babar entered Samarkand three times in 1497, 1501 and 1511. Each time he was driven off by the Khan's troops after a short occupation. After his second failure in 1501, Babar turned south, yielding his kingdom of Farghana. He led his followers across the Hindu Kush Mountains and arrived in Kabul (present-day Afghanistan) in 1504. Following a last entry to Samarkand, and quick defeat by the Uzbek Turks, he returned to Kabul and spent five years pondering his next move.

Having studied the paintings of Tamerlane's campaign against Delhi in 1398, Babar decided to move into northern India. By 1520, he had acquired some European matchlock shoulder muskets and a few pieces of artillery. Babar had the only cannons east of the Caspian Sea region.

Babar and his troops entered the **Khyber Pass** in December 1525. They entered the area known as **Hindustan** (the Ganges Plain of northern India) and soon were confronted by the forces of **Ibrahim Lodi**, the sultan of Delhi. The two armies met on the plain of Panipat on April 20, 1526. The sultan had 40,000 men to Babar's 25,000, but Babar's

Zahiruddin Mohammed Babar

entrenched infantry beat back attack after attack. Then, using their few firearms for shock value, Babar's men left their trenches and attacked. The sultan's army was routed and Ibrahim himself was killed.

Babar went on to defeat the forces of eight Rajput princes collected against him on the battlefield of Kanwaha (March 16, 1527). Then and there he broke the power of the Rajput confederacy. Having already subdued Delhi, he marched on to the confluence of the Gore River with the Ganges, where he defeated the Afghan rulers of Bihart and Bengal in May 1529. By the end of that year, Babar ruled the entire area from the highlands of Badakhishan to the Ganges River, much of present-day northern India.

Having acquired Persian tastes during his years in Kabul, Babar ordered a new capital built at Agra, and imported Persian architects to design the city. He died at Agra on December 26, 1530. *Tuzuk*, his autobiography, reveals him as an intelligent and humorous man, one given to literary pursuits and philosophy as well as the art of conquest.

43. Hernán Cortéz
(c. 1485–1547)

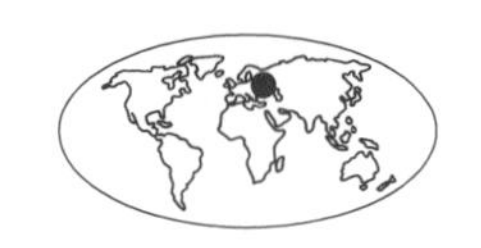

Hernán Cortéz was born in Medellin, Spain. In 1504, he crossed the Atlantic and became a notary and gentleman farmer on the island of **Hispaniola** (present-day Haiti and Dominican Republic). Cortéz participated in the Spanish conquest of **Cuba** (1511) and married Catalina Xuarez, the sister-in-law of Cuba's new governor. In 1518, he was named commander of an expedition intended to verify or disprove the rumors of an immensely wealthy Indian civilization on the mainland of Mexico.

Leaving Cuba with 11 ships and 600 men, Cortéz landed at present-day Veracruz on Good Friday in 1519. He marched inland and met and defeated the Tlaxacan tribe. Many of the Tlaxacans then joined Cortéz, because of their hatred of the Aztec tribe. Cortéz and his Spanish-Indian army arrived at the Aztec capital of Tenochtitlan on November 8, 1519. All the Spanish reports of that day describe it as a stunningly beautiful city, more than equal to the great European cities of that time.

The Aztec ruler **Montezuma** greeted the Spaniards in friendship. He was overawed by their firearms, swords and horses, none of which he had ever seen before. Seeing that the Aztecs feared his force, Cortéz abducted Montezuma and held him as a hostage to guarantee the good behavior of the Aztecs. Cortéz had to leave the city early in 1520 to meet and defeat a Spanish force sent to arrest him (the governor of Cuba had become suspicious of Cortéz's ambition). Cortéz then hastened back to Tenochtitlan and found open warfare between his men and the Aztec warriors. The Spaniards evacuated the city on the ***noche triste*** (night of sadness) of June 30, 1520, during which many soldiers on both sides were killed.

Cortéz recruited more Indian allies and besieged the city from May–August 1521. The Spaniards and their allies won the final battles and conquered the city. Cortéz then set up the government of **New Spain**, and Tenochtitlan was renamed **Mexico City**.

Cortéz built a great house at Cuernavaca and had some 20,000 Indians serve him as vassals.

Cortéz went to Spain in 1528 and returned with the title of Marquis, but not Viceroy as he had hoped. He made an abortive attempt to colonize in present-day California before he returned to Spain for good in 1540.

Hernán Cortéz

Though he had received many honors since his conquests, Cortéz never gained satisfaction from King Charles V. It is said that the desperate old soldier hung on to the resplendent coach of the king and begged him for recognition of his services. Cortéz died near Seville. His remains were later shipped to Mexico and buried in the land of New Spain, which he had done so much to create.

44. Suleiman I, the Magnificent
(1494–1566)

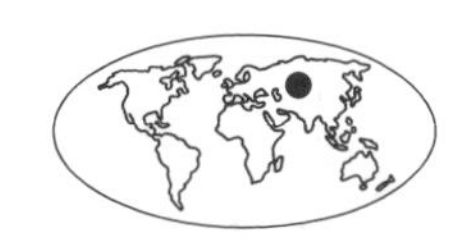

The greatest ruler, lawgiver and warrior of the Ottoman Empire, **Suleiman the Magnificent** was born in Trebizond, on the Black Sea. His father, a provincial governor, was elevated to become Sultan **Selim I**. Suleiman served as governor of Feodosia in the Crimea (1509–1512) and then the province of Magnesia, in western Turkey (1512–1520).

Learning of his father's death, Suleiman hastened to Istanbul (formerly Constantinople), where he was installed as sultan in 1520. Extremely ambitious for himself, the empire, and the Moslem cause, he began at once to make war on Christian Europe. Suleiman saw Emperor **Charles V** of Rome as his great rival in the quest to become the "ruler of the age."

Suleiman captured Belgrade from the Hungarians in 1521 and drove the **Knights of St. John** from the island of Rhodes in 1522. Both of these were landmark victories, since Suleiman's redoubtable grandfather, **Mehmed II, the Conqueror** (see no. 40), had been unable to accomplish them.

Suleiman defeated the Hungarian nation at the **Battle of Mohacs** (August 29, 1526), where King **Louis II** of Hungary and many of his nobles lost their lives. Feeling his strength, Suleiman pushed his army all the way to Vienna in 1529. The siege (September 23–October 16) was hard-fought on both sides, but some 16,000 Christian troops were able to repel the 80,000-man Turkish army. Furious over the defeat, Suleiman marched back to Istanbul.

Suleiman turned his attention to naval warfare in the Mediterranean. His formidable admiral, **Barbarossa** (Khair ed-Din), harassed Christian shipping from Turkey to Italy but was prevented from entering the western Mediterranean by the noble Knights of St. John, who had established a new base on the island of Malta. Meanwhile, Suleiman expanded eastward by land. He led his army all the way to Baghdad in 1534 and fought a long series of campaigns in the East before coming to peace terms with the Persians in 1555.

Suleiman I, the Magnificent

Turning his attention once more to Christian Europe, Suleiman sent his entire fleet west to attack Malta in 1566. Lacking the inspired leadership of Barbarossa, who had died in 1546, the Turks came close to success but time and again were thwarted by the desperate bravery of the knights and the rocky defenses of the island. The campaign ended in disaster, with 20,000 men and many ships lost. Suleiman vowed to avenge the defeat, but he died later in the same year.

45. The Duke of Alva
(1507–1583)

Fernando Alvarez de Toledo, "The Duke of Alva," was born in Piedrahita in Avila, a province in Spain. Known as "Alva," he came from a family of distinguished warriors. Alva's father was killed in battle when he was only three years old and he was reared by his grandfather.

Alva entered the Spanish army and fought the French at the siege of Fuenterrabia (1524). Alva won the attention of King **Charles I** of Spain, with whom he served in Italy and Hungary against the Ottoman Turks. Alva led the king's troops at the siege of Tunis in 1535, and led the abortive campaign against Moslem Algeria in 1541.

Named commander-in-chief of the Spanish armies fighting in Germany, Alva defeated **John Frederick**, the Protestant elector of Saxony, at the **Battle of Muhlberg** (1547). During a conflict between Alba's new sovereign, King **Philip II**, and the pope, Alva marched his men up to the gates of Rome, menacing the papal city until the pope and the king came to terms.

The Duke of Alva

King Philip II was a committed Catholic; he hated the new Protestant sects. He sent Alva as captain-general to the Netherlands (1567) with orders to put down a revolt there. Given the additional titles of governor and regent, Alva embarked on a rigorous oppression of the Calvinists in Holland. He founded the **Council of Troubles** (which the Calvinists called the "Council of Blood") and thousands of persons were condemned to death by it without any hope of appeal.

Alva defeated the Protestant leader **Louis of Nassau** at Jemmingen in 1568, and he forced **William the Silent** to leave the country and take refuge in Germany. Alva seemed on the verge of success when the Dutch formed an independence movement called the **Sea Beggars**. These coastal privateers harassed Alva's supply lines and promoted further rebellions in the Netherlands. Alva marched against his foes on land and defeated the Calvinists at Mons, Zutphen, Naarden and Haarlem (all in 1572), but the overall effect of his campaign was only to stiffen the resolve of the Protestant revolutionaries.

Seeing the failure of Alva's policy, Philip II recalled his general to Spain in 1573. Alva received a cool reception at Philip's palace, the Escorial, and he was exiled to his estates. He was recalled to service in 1580, when Philip invaded Portugal. Alva won the **Battle of the Bridge of Alcantara,** which won Portugal for Philip, but he received scant reward for his victory. Before he died at Lisbon in 1582, Alva made a statement about the relationship between soldiers and rulers that has a ring of truth: "Kings treat men like oranges. They go for the juice, and once they have sucked them dry, they throw them aside."

46. Oda Nobunaga
(1534–1582)

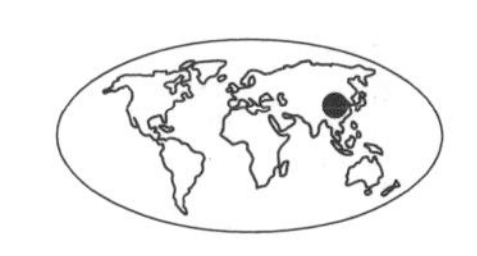

Japan in the 16th century was a land of small feudal principalities ruled by ***daimyos*** (lords) and a ***shogun*** in Kyoto who held much more power than the figurehead emperor. It was a period of unrestrained warfare in Japan. Into this mix stepped **Oda Nobunaga**.

Nobunaga's father was a minor daimyo in the province of Owari, east of Kyoto. Nobunaga succeeded to his father's position at the age of 16. He defeated his rival daimyo, **Imagawa Yoshimoto**, when the latter tried to enter the capital city of Kyoto in 1560. Nobunaga then entered an alliance with **Tokugawa Iyeyasu** (1542–1616). He expanded his power base through marriages and defeated other daimyos or won their allegiance.

Nobunaga conquered the large province of Mino in 1562 to 1564 and made an alliance with **Yoshiaki**, the younger brother of the recently assassinated shogun. Nobunaga occupied the city of Kyoto in 1568 under the pretext that it was in danger. He took the title of vice-shogun for himself, and when Yoshiaki tried to build an alliance of equals with him, Nobunaga drove him from the city. Nobunaga did not replace Yoshiaki, thereby ending the Ashikaga shogunate which had ruled Japan since 1338.

Having removed the last formal barrier to his own power, Nobunaga proceeded to build a castle on Lake Biwa. He welcomed Jesuit priests from Europe and traded with Portugal to import firearms, which made his power all the more unassailable. Nobunaga then turned against the **Buddhist** priests of his own country. His forces destroyed the vast Buddhist monastery at Enryaku, near Kyoto, and killed most of the monks there. He also captured the castle-monastery of Osaka; the True Pure Land Buddhist sect never recovered from the blows Nobunaga directed against it.

Nobunaga's greatest victory came at the **Battle of Nagashino** in 1573. His 30,000 troops met the 15,000-man army of **Takeda Katsuyri**. Nobunaga's opponent had by far the larger number of ***samurai*** cavalry, but Nobunaga defeated him by placing 3,000 of his best ***arquebusiers*** (musketmen) behind palisades. The gunfire caused great losses to Katsuyri's mounted forces.

By 1582, more than 150,000 Japanese had accepted Christianity, a situation Nobunaga had encouraged. He controlled 32 of the 68 provinces of Japan at the time of his death. He was assassinated by the same Buddhist retainer whom he had ordered to destroy Mount Hiei.

Oda Nobunaga

47. Francis Drake
(c. 1539–1596)

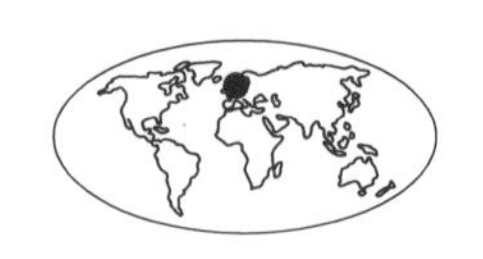

Francis Drake

England's greatest Elizabethan military leader, was born at Crowndale in the west county of Devon. His father was a tenant farmer and lay preacher of the new reformed Protestant faith. Sir **Frances Drake** grew up amid the turbulence of religious dissension. At the age of 13, he was apprenticed to the master of a coastal vessel.

Drake took to the sea as if born to it, and his aged master left the ship to him in his will. At 23, Drake enlisted in the fleet of the Hawkins family of Plymouth. He sailed on two voyages to the **Spanish West Indies** (Caribbean). When the second trip ended in disaster in 1572, Drake began a lifelong hatred of the Spaniards. He believed they were treacherous, as well as heretics.

Drake received a privateer's commission from Queen **Elizabeth I** in 1572, which allowed him to attack enemy ships and keep their cargoes. He and his company of 73 men sailed to the West Indies in two small ships. Drake plundered the important Spanish town of **Nombre de Dios** in Panama and crossed the **Isthmus of Panama** on foot to see the Pacific Ocean. He was probably the first Englishman to do this.

This first major success led to the greatest endeavor of his life — the circumnavigation of the globe. Drake sailed from England in December 1577 with 200 men aboard five ships. The expedition wintered in **Patagonia**, and Drake led his fleet through the hazardous **Strait of Magellan** from August 21 to September 6, 1578. Having navigated the strait, Drake and his men became the first Englishmen ever to sail on the Pacific.

Drake pillaged town after town on the west coast of South America. He sailed north and refitted his ships on the coast of what he called **New Albion** (present-day California). He went home by way of the Moluccan Islands, the Indian Ocean, and Cape of Good Hope. Drake reached Plymouth, England on September 26, 1580. He was celebrated for his victories, and the Queen knighted him aboard his flagship, the *Golden Hind,* as a reward for his voyage and victories.

In 1587, Drake led an English force into the Spanish harbor of Cadiz. He sacked and burned as many as 20 ships, thereby delaying the sailing of the great **Spanish Armada** by a full year. He called this action "singeing the king of Spain's beard."

Drake was vice-admiral of the English fleet in 1588, second in command to Lord **Howard of Effingham**. It was Drake who led the dauntless English attacks against the huge galleons of the Armada and he who proposed the use of "fire ships" (ships filled with explosives, set afire, and floated into the enemy) against the Spanish at their harbor in Calais.

Sadly, his career did not end with success. Drake and John Hawkins sailed to the West Indies in 1595–1596. The English fleet lost men and morale due to an epidemic of fever. Drake himself succumbed on January 28, 1596; he was buried at sea off Puerto Bello, Panama.

48. Maurice of Nassau
(1567–1625)

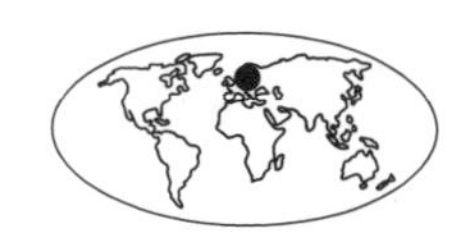

Maurice of Nassau, the Prince of Orange and second son of **William I** (the Silent), was born the same year as the start of the Netherlands War of Independence. After his father was assassinated by agents of King **Philip II** of Spain in 1584; Philip's troops proceeded to capture the Dutch provinces of Flanders and Brabant.

Nassau was named ***stadholder*** (hereditary magistrate) of the Dutch Republic's seven allied northern provinces, sharing power with **Johan Oldenbarneveldt**, the Landsadvocaat of Holland, the wealthiest and most powerful of the provinces. After an English attempt to intervene on behalf of the Dutch failed, Nassau became the center of Dutch hopes for independence from Spain. He was named captain-general of the army of the **United Provinces of the Netherlands** in 1590.

Johan Oldenbarneveldt

Nassau's education at the University of Leiden served him well. He developed a new type of army. Basing his approach on classic Roman treatises, Nassau made drill and organization the centerpieces of Dutch army training. The Dutch troops were formed into shallow units, 10 ranks deep, which allowed for mobility and precise maneuvers. Under the leadership of the Nassau family, the Dutch soldiers became renowned for their ability to break ranks and then reform them at twice the speed of other armies. Nassau also incorporated scientific principles of engineering, relying on trench warfare, long-range siege gunnery and mines.

Nassau fought a series of campaigns against the Spanish armies led by the **Duke of Parma** and **Ambrogio di Spinola**. Although the Spanish formations had been the terror of Europe, Nassau — with an army of 10,000 men — liberated **Breda** (his family seat) in 1590. The following year, Nassau defeated the Spanish at the **Siege of Zutphen** in seven days, the **Siege of Deventer** in 11 days, and the **Siege of Nijmegan** in six days. These victories led up to the largest pitched battle of the war, the **Battle of Nieuport**, which Nassau won in 1600.

From 1609 to 1621, the Twelve Years' Truce halted the war between the Netherlands and Spain. During this period of peace, Nassau maintained a standing Dutch army of 30,000 infantry and 3,600 mounted soldiers.

By 1617, Nassau, an Orthodox Calvinist, came into open conflict with Oldenbarneveldt who represented the burghers, whose power, in the absence of a sovereign, was formidable. An impending religious civil war was averted when Nassau had Oldenbarnevelt executed in 1619.

Nassau became prince of Orange after the death of his older brother in 1618. When war with Spain resumed, his younger half-brother, Frederick Henry, liberated more Dutch cities (1625–1647) while Admiral **Maarten von Tromp** (see no. 51) dominated Spain on the seas. The United Provinces would win their full independence from Spain 23 years after Nassau's death more by their strength on water than by land power.

49. Albrecht von Wallenstein (1583–1634)

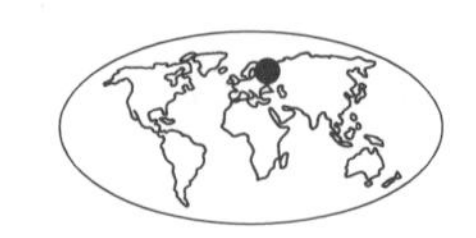

Albrecht Wensel Eusebius von Wallenstein was born in Hermanic, Bohemia (today the Czech Republic). Son of a noble Bohemian family, he was orphaned at the age of 13. He converted from Lutheranism to Catholicism in 1606, but his true belief was in astrology. He treasured an astrological horoscope compiled for him by the famous astronomer **Johannes Kepler**. The start of the Bohemian revolt against the **Holy Roman Empire** (1618–1623) provided him with the opportunity to fully develop his military talents.

The fighting that began in Bohemia spread to much of Europe and became known as the **Thirty Years' War** (1618–1648). Von Wallenstein recruited thousands of soldiers to fight under his command. He also made loans to Emperor **Ferdinand II** of Rome. By 1623, von Wallenstein was the wealthiest man in Bohemia, and he had confiscated the lands and estates of many Protestant nobles. He consolidated his position through his marriage in 1623 to a daughter of Count **von Harrackh**, one of the emperor's closest advisers.

The Thirty Years' War entered its second phase in 1625 when Protestant Denmark joined the fray. Von Wallenstein won the **Battle of Dessau Bridge** and advanced all the way to the Baltic Sea. Granted the title of General of the North and Baltic Seas, he was at the very height of his power when the established German nobles forced Ferdinand II to dismiss him in 1630; they were envious of his power and success.

Von Wallenstein immediately began to correspond with **Gustavus Adolphus** (see no. 50), the Lutheran king of Sweden, who had joined the war on the Protestant side. Adolphus spurned his offer of service, and von Wallenstein was lucky to be recalled by Ferdinand II in 1631.

Battle of Dessau Bridge

The two great leaders of the war — von Wallenstein and Adolphus — met at the **Battle of Lutzen** in 1632. Von Wallenstein had almost 15,000 men and 21 heavy cannon, but 3,000 of his men were not present for the early part of the fighting. Adolphus led 16,300 men and approximately 60 cannon, as well as new fighting formations that von Wallenstein was unfamiliar with. The battle was a near draw and was governed by chance in its later stages. The Swedes won the day, but Adolphus was killed in the fighting.

Von Wallenstein planned a revolt against Ferdinand II during 1633. Learning of this, the emperor ordered von Wallenstein brought to him, dead or alive. The scheming commander was assassinated at Eger, Bohemia, by **Walter Devereux**, an English captain, on February 25, 1634. His life and career were commemorated in a dramatic trilogy by the German poet **Johann von Schiller**.

50. Gustavus Adolphus II
(1594–1632)

Gustavus Adolphus was born in Stockholm in 1594, the son of King **Charles IX** of Sweden. He became king in his own right in 1611. Due to his youth — he was only 17 — he had to make a number of concessions to the Swedish nobles. He thereby won their loyalty, something he needed since the country would be at war during nearly the entire period he was on the throne.

Adolphus fought against Denmark (1611–1613) and lost. He fought against Russia (1613–1617) and succeeded in excluding that country from the Baltic Sea area. This had implications for future Swedish-Russian relations (see nos. 56 and 57). Adolphus fought between 1621 and 1629. He captured the important city of **Riga** and concluded a truce with his enemies.

During his wars with Denmark, Russia and Poland, Adolphus thoroughly reformed his army. By compiling a roster of all Swedish men over the age of 15 and using a **draft** (the men were "drafted" into military service), he created the first **national army** in modern Europe. Most armies of the time were composed of mercenaries (hired killers without loyalty to the leaders they served).

He studied the Spanish ***tercio*** and improved upon it, establishing squadrons of 216 pikemen and 192 musketeers formed in ranks that were only six men deep. Two or three squadrons joined together made a battle group or brigade. Adolphus formed his cavalry in groups that were only three ranks deep; the cavalry trained to charge at a trot and to use swords and pistols at close quarters. Finally, Adolphus changed the artillery, making it much lighter and faster; his troops were probably the first Europeans to employ the three-pounder cannon.

Adolphus brought this effective combination of infantry, cavalry and artillery across the Baltic Sea to Germany in June 1630. A devout Lutheran, he entered the **Thirty Years' War** to aid the Protestant cause. The Swedes took up a strong position in northern Germany, but were attacked by the Imperial Catholic forces at Breitenfeld in 1631. Adolphus's victory there won him the nicknames "**Lion of the North**" and "**Savior of Protestantism.**"

He campaigned in southern Germany in the spring of 1632 and captured Munich in May. On November 6, 1632, Adolphus led 16,000 men in the **First Battle of Lutzen** against the Catholic troops of **Albrecht von Wallenstein** (see no. 49), who had perfected the use of mercenary soldiers. The Swedes won the battle, but Adolphus was killed in the fighting with shots through his head, side, arm and back. Wallenstein left 3,000 men dead on the field in his first major setback of the war.

Gustavus Adolphus' death at Lutzen

51. Maarten von Tromp
(1597–1653)

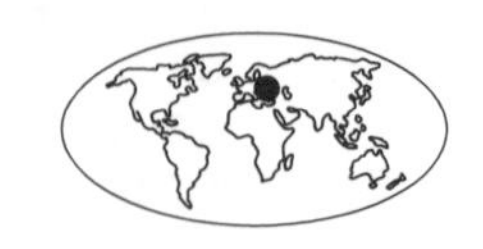

The greatest admiral of the 17th century Dutch navy was **Maarten Harpertszoon von Tromp**. He was born in Breille, Holland, the son of the captain of a small Dutch ship. The **United Provinces of the Netherlands** (of which Holland was one) were fighting for their freedom from Spain, and Tromp accompanied his father on a voyage, during which his father was killed in an encounter with an English pirate ship. Tromp swore vengeance on all the enemies of his country.

After sailing in the Dutch merchant marine, Tromp entered the Dutch navy in 1624 as captain of a frigate. He showed great resolve in the face of danger and rose rapidly through the ranks to become a lieutenant admiral in 1637.

Tromp fought against the Spanish and defeated their fleet in the North Sea off the Dutch coast at Gravelines (February 18, 1639). Later in the year, Spain sent an enormous fleet against the Dutch. Tromp had 31 ships to send against 67 Spanish vessels, one of which, the *Mater Theresa*, was the largest warship in the world at that time.

Urged by his lieutenants to exercise prudence, Tromp declared, "There is room enough at the bottom of the sea for all those Spanish ships, and the sooner we start sending them there, the better." As good as his word, Tromp led a midnight attack and threw the Spanish fleet into confusion. After taking refuge behind a sandbar on the English coast, the Spanish tried to make a run for the port of Dunkirk (approximately 15 miles northeast of Gravelines). Tromp then delivered a death blow to Spanish sea power, capturing or sinking all but 18 ships in their fleet in the **Battle of the Downs**.

Tromp fought against the English in the **First English-Dutch War** (1652–1654). He won a major victory over English Admiral **Robert Blake** at the **Battle of Dungeness** in the winter of 1652. The two-day naval battle gave the Dutch temporary control of the **English Channel**.

Maarten von Tromp

Early in 1653, The English and Dutch waged and split two more battles at sea. The **Battle of North Foreland I** was fought to a draw and the **Battle of Portland** was won by England.

In the summer of 1653, English Admiral **George Monck** engaged Tromp off the Dutch island of Textel near the coast of Scheveningen. Both sides had approximately 120 ships positioned in rough line-ahead formations across 16 miles of the North Sea. This **Battle of Textel I** was the greatest naval battle fought to date. The two navies battled without decision until the following day, when, Monck, reinforced by fresh ships, resumed the attack and defeated the Dutch.

During the battle, Tromp was struck in the chest by musket fire and killed. The fleet lost 20 of its 100 ships through capture or sinking as the heart went out of the Dutch navy with the death of its greatest commander.

52. Oliver Cromwell
(1599–1658)

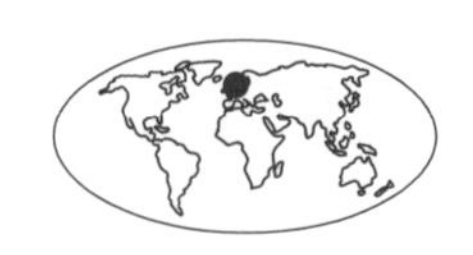

The only true dictator in England's history was born in Huntingdon in 1599. **Oliver Cromwell** attended Sydney Sussex College at Cambridge. Influenced by his university years and by a deep personal depression in his late 20s, Cromwell became a devout Puritan. Puritanism was the minority faith in England at the time; the official national church was Anglican.

Cromwell was elected to **Parliament** in 1640. Following the lead of his relative **John Hampden**, who had resisted King **Charles I**'s "ship money" tax, he joined the Parliamentary party. When the **English Civil War** broke out in 1643, Cromwell became a colonel and then a lieutenant-general in the **Roundhead** (Parliamentary) cavalry.

For a man who never saw military service until after he was 40, Cromwell evolved into a remarkable military leader. He smashed the **Cavalier** (Royalist) cavalry at the **Battle of Marston Moor** in northern England in 1644. Returning to London, he was instrumental in creating the "**New Model Army**:" 12 infantry regiments, 10 cavalry regiments and one of dragoons. Cromwell was second in command to Sir **Thomas Fairfax**.

Oliver Cromwell

Cromwell's New Model cavalry regiments won the crucial **Battle of Naseby** on June 14, 1645. Although the English Civil War had ended, King Charles I continued to conspire with Scotland to regain his throne. Cromwell initiated the action of the **Second Civil War** (1648–1651) by marching north and defeating the Scots at the **Battle of Preston**. Then he crossed the Irish Sea, landed in Ireland, and defeated the Catholic forces there. Cromwell's soldiers carried out two horrendous massacres of Irish soldiers and civilians at **Drogheda** and **Wexford**.

Cromwell dominated the Parliamentary trial that condemned King Charles I to death in 1649. He marched north in 1650 and won an overwhelming victory against the Scots at the **Battle of Dunbar** (September 3, 1650). Cromwell followed this with a victory at the **Battle of Worcester** (September 3, 1651) that ended the Second Civil War.

Having attained peace, though not unity, Cromwell became the dictator of the British Isles. He expelled the "Rump" Parliament in 1653 and was installed as "Lord Protector." In 1655, he created 11 military districts throughout England, each one governed by a major-general from his forces.

Extremely ambitious in his foreign policy, Cromwell fought both the Spanish and the Dutch during the 1650s. English forces took Jamaica from Spain and intervened in the long-standing war between France and Spain. Cromwell's foreign policy roused the British lion in a manner that had not been seen since the days of Sir **Francis Drake** (see no. 47).

Cromwell died at Whitehall on September 3, 1658, the anniversary of two of his greatest victories. He was buried in King **Henry VII**'s chapel at **Westminster Abbey** with all due ceremony. But when King **Charles II** ascended the throne in 1660 (an event known as the "**Restoration**"), Cromwell's bones were disinterred and hung on a gallows at Tyburn.

53. Louis II de Bourbon (1621–1686)

Louis II of the **House of Bourbon** was born in Paris. He became the leader of his family, a junior branch of the royal house of Bourbon. The Conde (the title means "prince") was educated by Jesuit teachers, and he married Mademoiselle de Maille-Breze in 1641; she was a niece of Cardinal **Richelieu,** the chief minister to King **Louis XIII.**

Due to his family standing and marriage, the Conde was given command of the royal army of France in 1643. In that critical year, late in the **Thirty Years' War,** he won an overwhelming victory against the Spanish at the **Battle of Rocroi.** Louis combined the use of cavalry and musketeers to defeat the famed Spanish ***tercios,*** who had been nearly unbeaten on the battlefield since the early 16th century. In one day of fighting, the Conde ended Spanish power in northern Europe and elevated France to the rank of first power in Europe.

Following the deaths of both King Louis XIII and Cardinal Richelieu, the Conde served King **Louis XIV** and Cardinal **Jules Mazarin.** He led a brilliant campaign in the Netherlands in 1646 and won a great victory at **Lens** in 1648.

The Conde took the side of the aristocratic rebels during the **Fronde of the Princes** (1651–1652). This rebellion collapsed in 1652, and he fled the country to join the forces of King **Philip IV** of Spain in the Netherlands. Condemned as a traitor and sentenced to death in his absence, the Conde fought with the Spanish until the **Treaty of the Pyrenees** ended the **Franco-Spanish War** in 1659.

Remarkably, the Conde was restored to his lands, states and titles, and the condemnation and sentence were removed. King Louis XIV was reluctant to entrust a great command to the former rebel, but in 1668, the Conde led a campaign into the area of **Franche-Comte.**

Louis II de Bourbon, the Great Conde

His performance was good enough to earn him a promotion.

In 1672, the Conde led the French army in its famous crossing of the Rhine at the start of the **French-Dutch War** (1672–1676). He was wounded in the crossing, and his battle actions caused him to lose the confidence of the king. The Conde was more cautious than in his early years; he missed a chance to defeat the Dutch at the **Battle of Seneffe** (1674). His last days in battle were spent in a campaign to defend the province of Alsace from attack (1675).

The great commander then retired to his estate at Chantilly and lived the life of a country gentleman. He died at Fountainbleau, after having sent a letter to King Louis XIV asking the monarch to forgive his actions during the period of the Fronde.

54. Sebastien le Prestre de Vauban
(1633–1707)

Sebastien le Prestre de Vauban was born at St. Legerde-Fougeret in the province of Burgundy, France. Educated by the Carmelite order of nuns, he became a cadet in the regiment of **Louis II de Bourbon, the Great Conde** (see no. 53). De Vauban fought with the Conde against the troops of King **Louis XIV** for two years. After he was captured in 1653, and was well-treated by his captors, de Vauban switched sides in the **Fronde of the Princes**, a rebellion of the French nobles. He joined King Louis XIV's army, where he would spend most of the rest of his life.

De Vauban's entire generation was appalled by the high casualties suffered during the **Thirty Years' War** (1618–1648). Seeking an enlightened alternative to field warfare, de Vauban became the foremost proponent of siege warfare, the building and taking of large-scale fortresses. He became a royal engineer (1655), then commissary general of fortifications (1667), and in 1672, he persuaded the king to create a special engineering branch of the French royal army.

The **French-Dutch War** began in that same year. De Vauban captured the Dutch fortress of **Maastricht** in 1673 by laying out a complete set of siege parallels, earthworks that approached the fort by angles and turns. After the war ended, he built the fortress that guarded **Strasbourg** (1684) and directed the siege of **Luxembourg** (1684).

Already the acknowledged master of his art, de Vauban went on to introduce the use of ricochet gunfire in 1688; these were cannonballs that bounced over parapets and hit several parts of the enemy's defenses. He advocated the use of the socket bayonet, which could remain on the barrel of the musket while the gun was fired.

The **War of the League of Augsburg** brought de Vauban fully into his element. He captured Mons (1691) and Namur (1692) in the Netherlands and was wounded at the **Siege of Ath** (1697). His construction of fortifications enabled France to fight the combined powers of England, the Netherlands and Austria to a draw.

The start of the **War of Spanish Succession** in 1702 found France in a weaker position. De Vauban asked for, and received, promotion to marshal of France (1703). He directed the **Siege of Alt-Breisach** in 1703 and organized an entrenched camp at Dunkerque (1706). Other than that, his services were not called upon in a war that strayed from the principles of enlightened combat. Casualties in the war were shockingly high because of the change from the matchlock to flintlock musket.

De Vauban was an indefatigable worker. He wrote *On Siege and Fortification*, which was published many years after his death. He also wrote the controversial *Project for a Royal Tythe, or General Tax* (1707). During his 54 years in the service of the king, he had erected or designed 160 fortresses and participated in the sieges of 50 others.

Sebastien le Prestre de Vauban

55. John Churchill
(1650–1722)

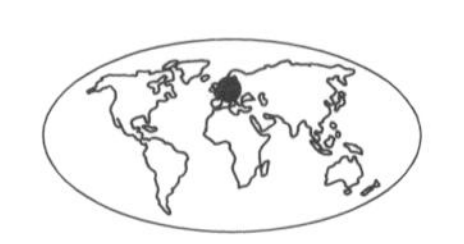

John Churchill was born at Ashe in Devonshire. His father had supported King **Charles I** during the **English Civil War**. Churchill took advantage of his sister's affair with **James, the Duke of York**, to advance his early career. He became a page to the Duke, was commissioned in the English army in 1668, and served in Tangier, Africa (1669–1670).

Churchill served in the army of France's King **Louis XIV** during a time of peace between the two countries in the 1670s. Having gained valuable experience, he returned to England and married Sarah Jennings, a 17-year-old attendant to Princess Anne (one of James' daughters). After the Duke of York became King **James II** in 1685, Churchill rose rapidly through the ranks.

Churchill changed sides in 1688. He deserted James II for **William of Orange** during the **Glorious Revolution**. When William became King **William III** in 1689, he made Churchill the Earl of Marlborough in gratitude. When William died, he was replaced on the throne by Queen **Anne** in 1702. (By this time, Sarah Churchill had become chief lady-in-waiting to the queen.)

Queen Anne made Churchill master-general of ordnance (artillery) and captain-general of the English army in 1702. She also elevated his title from earl to the Duke of Marlborough. Churchill took command of the allied English-Dutch army in the Netherlands. He initiated a series of campaigns that led to brilliant victories at **Blenheim** (1704), **Ramillies** (1706) and **Oudenaarde** (1708). In that same year, he captured the great citadel at **Lille** by constructing an outside series of fortifications so intricate it could not be penetrated by the relieving French army.

Duke of Marlborough

Churchill won his battles through a combination of technology and maneuvers. His troops were armed with the new flintlock (as opposed to the old-style matchlock) musket. Churchill saw that this change gave the advantage to the offense and he led his men in daring attacks that threw the enemy into confusion. He was also a master of siege warfare and defensive fighting, tactics he had probably learned during his years in the French service.

During his years as leader of the allied armies, Churchill won five battles and conducted 26 sieges, all of which were successful. He was probably the greatest military genius in the history of modern England.

Churchill and his wife fell out of Queen Anne's favor, and he was dismissed in 1711. He went to Europe and sought to persuade **George, the Elector of Hanover**, to invade England and establish a new monarchy. George crossed the channel peacefully and was soon installed as King **George I** of England. The new king restored Churchill to all his titles and honors, but a paralytic stroke in 1716 forced his retirement. He died at Windsor. His wife survived him by 23 years and occupied the palace of Blenheim, constructed to honor Churchill's greatest victory.

56. Peter the Great
(1672–1725)

Pyotr Alekseyevich was born in Moscow in 1672, the son of Czar **Alexis**. The rivalry between the Miloslavsky and Naryshkin clans, led by the czar's first and second wives respectively, shaped Peter's childhood and youth. After the death of his father, Peter was made co-czar with his half-brother **Ivan**, but the real power went to his half-sister **Sophia**, who ruled as regent. Peter lived in fear of the ***streltsy***, the royal bodyguards who served his half-sister.

In 1689, Peter took advantage of a revolt by the streltsy to remove his sister from power, and he banished her to a convent. After the death of Ivan in 1696, Peter took the throne as sole czar and proceeded to change Russia.

Peter wanted to modernize his country. Russia had no navy, no ports, and no trade or exchange with other European countries. Seeking to change this, Peter initiated a war with the Ottoman Turks for control of the region north of the Black Sea. His campaign won control of the Don River, giving him a route to the Mediterranean.

Wanting to know more about western Europe, Peter went incognito to visit most of the major European nations during 1696 and 1697. The towering czar — he was six feet seven inches tall — looked out of place as he went to Austria, France, the Netherlands and England. Peter worked as a ship's carpenter in Holland and saw the great advantages held by the European nations in arms and armaments.

Peter the Great

Peter returned to Russia in 1698 and began a war against Sweden, which held Karelia, Ingria, Estonia and Livonia, all the lands Peter wanted Russia to possess on the edge of the Baltic Sea.

The **Great Northern War** (1700–1721) began badly for Russia. The Swedish leader, King **Charles XII** (see no. 57), was a military genius who defeated the Russians at Narva (1700). Peter had to change the very model of the Russian army, employing architects and engineers to bring in artillery and train his men. Peter then captured **Narva** in a siege (1704) and won the **Battle of Lesnaya** (1708).

His most important victories came at **Poltava** (1709) and the naval **Battle of Gangut**, where the Swedish monopoly of the Baltic Sea was broken. The **Treaty of Nystad** (1721) gave the eastern shores of the Baltic to Russia, which finally had what Peter referred to as the "window to the West." The city of **Saint Petersburg** was built to complete his success on Russia's northwestern front.

Peter changed his title from czar to **imperator** (emperor) of all the Russias in 1721. He died in 1725, leaving a far stronger Russia than he had found when he came to the throne.

57. Charles XII
(1682–1718)

A brilliant and impulsive man, **Charles XII** led his Swedish troops to many victories but was unable to stem the tide of Russia's growing power. Born in Stockholm in 1682, Charles received an excellent education prior to his ascension to the throne at the age of 15. He enjoyed two short years of peace before Russia, Saxony-Poland, and Denmark jointly declared war on his nation.

Sweden had been the dominant nation on the shores of the Baltic Sea since the time of **Gustavus Adolphus** (see no. 50). Charles had no intention of relinquishing this position. He mustered the small but professional Swedish army and started the war by invading Denmark. He swiftly overcame the Danes and won peace through the **Treaty of Travendal**. Then he marched eastward and attacked the Russian army of **Peter the Great** (see no. 56) that was besieging Narva. The Swedes attacked in a snowstorm at night and thoroughly defeated the Russians. The Swedes suffered 2,000 casualties, the Russians between 8,000 and 10,000.

Having deterred the Russian threat temporarily, Charles turned his attention to Poland, which he believed was the key to eastern Europe. He marched through Poland and ousted King **Augustus** from power. Charles then set his sights again on Russia, where Czar Peter the Great had reformed his army and was threatening Swedish control of the Baltic Sea.

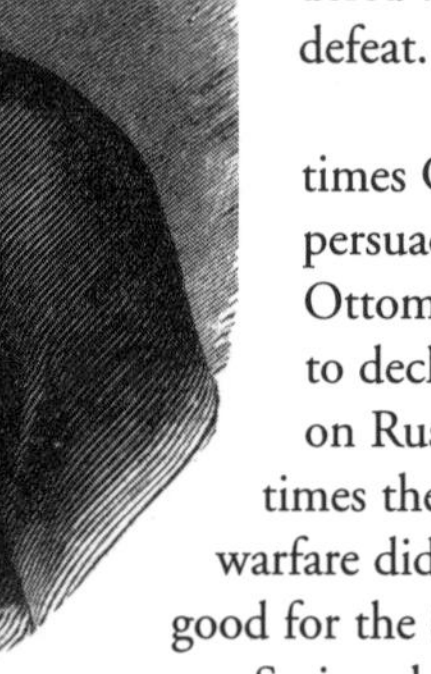

Charles XII

Charles invaded the Russian Ukraine. He marched as far as Poltava, where he was met by a larger Russian army led by the czar. Charles lost the critical **Battle of Poltava** (1709). He fled south from the battlefield and took up a residence in exile under the protection of the Ottoman Turks. Most of the men he had brought into Russia surrendered after the defeat.

Three times Charles persuaded the Ottoman sultan to declare war on Russia; three times the ensuing warfare did little good for the Swedish cause. Seeing this, Charles rode incognito across Europe and reached Sweden in 1714. He gathered his largest army to date — 80,000 men — and set out to regain the borders Sweden had lost. He was killed by a bullet through the head while besieging the Norwegian fortress of **Frederiksten** in December 1718.

The "boy king" had fought ferociously for his kingdom. Had he gathered more allies to his cause, he might well have prevailed, given his strategic insights and personal charisma.

58. Frederick II
(1712–1786)

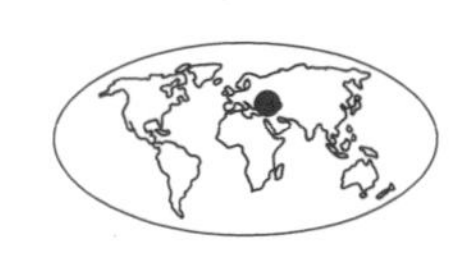

The third Hohenzollern king of Prussia was born in Berlin in 1712. Son of King **Frederick William I** and Princess **Sophia** of Hanover, **Frederick the Great** grew up in a tense and combative household. His father suffered from illness and berated his son publicly while in a rage. Frederick once ran away from home with his best friend. The pair was apprehended, and Frederick had the misfortune of seeing his friend publicly executed.

When his father died, Frederick ascended to the throne in 1740, the same year that Emperor **Charles VI** of Austria died, leaving the throne to his daughter, **Maria Theresa**. Sensing that Europe would soon burst into a general conflagration of war, Frederick seized the initiative and declared war on Austria. His crack Prussian army quickly seized the wealthy Austrian province of Silesia.

The resulting **War of the Austrian Succession** (1740–1748) tilted back and forth. Frederick changed allies and enemies with duplicitous ease, thereby winning a reputation for fraud. When the war ended in 1748, he still held Silesia, but had won the undying enmity of Maria Theresa, who gathered Czarina **Elizabeth** of Russia and **Madame de Pompadour** of France as future allies.

Frederick flirted with the ambitious new thought of the **Enlightenment**. He brought the French satirist **Voltaire** to Berlin and wrote poetry himself. It would be difficult for the other European leaders to reconcile this cultured individual with the ruthless military leader they confronted in the **Seven Years' War** (1756–1763).

Attacked on land by France, Russia and Austria, Frederick had only Britain, a naval power, for an ally. He fought relentlessly and well, winning great victories at **Leuthen** and **Rossbach** (both in 1757). He also came back from resounding defeats at **Kolin** (1757) and **Kunersdorf** (1759). Berlin itself was briefly occupied by the Russian cavalry, but Frederick fought on until all the opposing powers were exhausted. He and Prussia were saved by the death of Czarina Elizabeth in 1762. Her successor, Czar **Peter III**, took Russia out of the war and gave Frederick much-needed breathing space. The **Treaty of Hubertsberg** (1763) confirmed the gains Prussia had made in 1740–1748.

Frederick never went to war again. The efficiency of the Prussian war machine stood as an effective deterrent to war during his lifetime. He died after having caught a chill while reviewing his troops in a pouring rain.

Frederick the Great

59. John Burgoyne
(1722–1792)

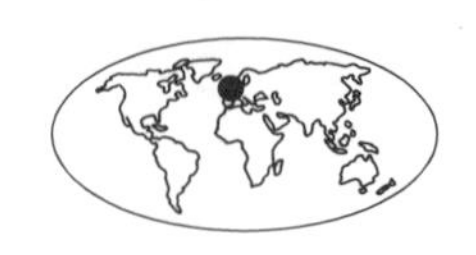

John Burgoyne was born in London, the son of a captain in the British army. He studied at the prestigious Westminster School. Burgoyne joined the army in 1740. He was given command of one of the new regiments of light cavalry commissioned in 1759. He made his military reputation during the British campaign in Portugal and Spain (1762–1763). He led his light cavalrymen on daring raids that brought him promotion to brigadier general.

Returning home again, Burgoyne ran for and won a seat in **Parliament** representing Midhurst in Sussex. He ran for election representing Preston, Lancashire, in 1768; he won the race and held that seat for the rest of his life.

In 1775, Burgoyne was sent to North America during the **Revolutionary War.** Promoted to major general, he witnessed the stirring **Battle of Bunker Hill** (1775) and came away convinced he could beat the Americans. After a frustrating campaign in Canada (1776), Burgoyne sought and obtained permission to lead a major invasion to capture and hold Albany, New York and the Hudson River Valley. This he believed was the key to winning the war.

Burgoyne led more than 7,000 British and Hessian troops south from Canada in June 1777. He adroitly positioned cannon on Mount Defiance and thereby captured **Fort Ticonderoga** on Lake Champlain. Rather than marching swiftly to Albany, Burgoyne pursued a slow route through the New York wilderness; his men averaged only one mile a day during July. When he did reach the Hudson River, he sent a large detachment of Hessian troops to find cattle and supplies; these men were nearly wiped out in August at the **Battle of Bennington** in Vermont.

John Burgoyne

Burgoyne should have retreated to Canada when he learned that General **William Howe** had gone south to Philadelphia, Pennsylvania, rather than advance north along the Hudson River to Albany. Instead, Burgoyne gambled and marched south, straight into a trap laid by 20,000 American militiamen led by Generals **Horatio Gates** and **Benedict Arnold.** Outnumbered and outfought at the battles of **Freeman's Farm** and **Bemis Heights**, Burgoyne tried to retreat but was surrounded. On October 17, 1777, he and more than 6,000 soldiers laid down their arms to the Americans in the **Convention of Saratoga.**

It was a stunning blow to the British side. France saw the opportunity to take revenge on Britain and entered the war as an ally of the Americans. Burgoyne himself was paroled to England in 1778. He was widely criticized for his surrender, but retained his seat in Parliament. He died in London and was buried in Westminster Abbey.

60. James Wolfe
(1727–1759)

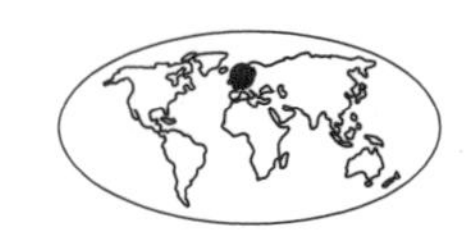

James Wolfe was born in Westerham, in Kent, England. He joined the British army as a commissioned officer in 1741.

This was an inglorious time for the British with the **Jacobite Rebellion.** Wolfe's career only began to blossom after the campaign that ended with the **Battle of Culloden** (1746). In the wake of **Bonnie Prince Charlie**'s failed effort to retake the throne, Wolfe fought remorselessly against the remnants of the Scottish clans, hunting down all the Jacobite supporters he could find. Ruthlessness remained an integral aspect of Wolfe's career and his character.

When the **Seven Years' War** began, **William Pitt**, (who became Britain's foreign minister), was convinced that the way to defeat France was to win the war at sea and capture her colonies in North America and the Caribbean. Pitt sent an enormous fleet and 16,000 men under Lord **Jeffrey Amherst** to capture the French fortress of Louisbourg, on the eastern coast of Cape Breton Island. Wolfe was sent as second in command.

Wolfe asserted himself boldly during the siege. He personally led a daring landing under full fire from French cannons and muskets at Kennington Cove. The British established a virtual city of their own to house and feed the troops during the seven-week siege of Louisbourg. When the enemy capitulated on July 20, it was a vindication of Wolfe and his particular breed of stubbornness. Hearing from one of his ministers that Wolfe must be mad, King **George II** replied "Mad, is he? Then I hope he will bite some of my other generals."

In June 1759, Wolfe and 9,000 troops were brought up the St. Lawrence River to Quebec City by Admiral **Charles Saunders**. Wolfe spent weeks reconnoitering and seeking a chink in the defenses of the French who were led by the **Marquis de Montcalm**. In early September, he discovered that the **Plains of Abraham**, only one mile south of the city, were guarded by just 100 men. During the night of September 12–13, 1759, Wolfe brought 5,000 troops by boat to Anse de Foulon, the cove at the river's edge. The British climbed the heights in darkness, overpowered the tiny garrison, and had 5,000 men and even some small artillery pieces on the plains by early morning.

Montcalm was both amazed and distressed by the British move. Rather than coordinate movements with French troops just 10 miles to the south, Montcalm chose to attack immediately. The British waited until the French were within 40 yards, then they released two devastating volleys of gunfire that routed Montcalm's men. Wolfe fell with three bullet wounds, however. His death on the plains was commemorated in a famous painting by **Benjamin West**. The victory won Canada for the British crown.

James Wolfe

61. Aleksandr Suvorov
(1729–1800)

Russia's great 18th-century commander was born in Moscow, four years after the death of Czar **Peter the Great** (see no. 56). **Aleksandr Suvorov** enrolled in the Semenovskii Life Guards in 1742 as a private. He worked his way up to sergeant (1751) and was commissioned an officer in 1754 at the age of 24.

Suvorov became a captain at the start of the **Seven Years' War** (1756) and rose to lieutenant colonel by 1758. He played a prominent role in the dramatic capture of **Berlin** in 1760 and distinguished himself in small cavalry actions in the following year. After Russia changed sides in 1762 (following the death of Czarina **Elizabeth**), Suvorov fought the Poles as colonel of the Astrakhan infantry regiment.

Switching military fronts, Suvorov then fought with Russia's Danubian army against the Turks (1768–1774). Russia had little success against the Turks until Suvorov arrived and took command. He won great victories at **Hirsov** and **Kozludji**, and at last the Turks sued for peace on terms acceptable to Czarina **Catherine the Great** (who had replaced Czar **Peter III** in 1762).

Aleksandr Suvorov

Even more important was Suvorov's campaign within Russia itself. **Emeleyan Pugachev**, a disaffected Cossack, led a full-scale revolt against Czarina Catherine, and it was Suvorov who brought the rebel back to Moscow in an iron cage. (Pugachev was tortured and killed at the czarina's order.)

To the Poles of his day, Suvorov was nothing less than a conqueror. When Poland fought against Russia, Suvorov captured **Krakow** (1772). He returned later and captured **Warsaw** (1794), thereby putting down the revolutionary and patriotic movement led by **Thaddeus Kosciuszko**.

Suvorov served with distinction in the second **Russo-Turkish War**. He won great victories at **Focsani** and **Rymnik** and captured the key Turkish fortress of **Izmail**, located on the Danube River. He was, by this time, the most experienced and successful military commander in all Europe. During a brief period of peace, he wrote *The Science of Victory*.

Suvorov had served four rulers (Elizabeth, Peter III, Catherine the Great and Paul I) during his remarkable career. He longed for an opportunity to meet Napoleon on the battlefield, but such was not to be the case. He died in 1800. His fame in Russia was later used for propaganda by Soviet dictator **Joseph Stalin**. During **World War II**, ghostly images of Suvorov appeared on recruitment posters, inciting Russians to strike at their foes once more.

62. George Washington
(1732–1799)

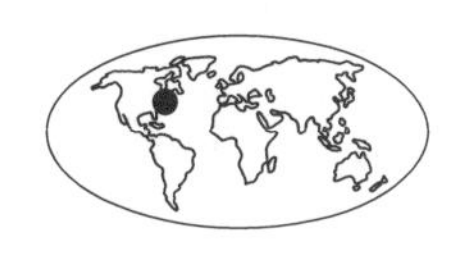

The "father of his country," **George Washington** was born in rural Virginia. From an early age, he yearned to distinguish himself in the British military service. His older half-brother, Lawrence Washington, served with the British-American expedition against Cartagena (1742) and named the family plantation **Mount Vernon** in honor of British admiral Edward Vernon.

George Washington became the adjutant of the Virginia colonial militia in 1752. He led Virginian troops in the ambush of the French ensign Jumonville that touched off the **French and Indian War** of 1754. The ambitious young British-American served as aide-de-camp to Britain's General **Braddock** (1755) and then worked to guard the Virginia frontier against Indian raids (1755–1758).

The start of the **Revolutionary War** altered his life forever. Washington was named commander-in-chief of the **Continental Army** in 1775 because he had more military experience than anyone in the colonies. The former British subject became a true American and went to Boston to assume command of the new army in July of that year. He would return to Mount Vernon only once during the entire course of the war.

George Washington

Washington sent Colonel **Henry Knox** on a mission to take cannons from **Fort Ticonderoga** to Massachusetts. Using this artillery, Washington forced the British to evacuate Boston in March 1776.

In December 1776, Washington crossed the **Delaware River** and surprised the Hessians (German mercenaries paid by the British) at **Trenton**. He proceeded to win again at **Princeton** in 1777, saving the colonial cause. He trained the amateur colonial forces well and shaped them into a disciplined army.

Washington endured notable losses at **Brandywine** and **Germantown** (both in 1777) and a frustrating draw **Battle at Monmouth** in 1778. During the latter, Washington's presence prevented a rout. Seeing the manner in which Washington conducted himself on the field that day, his French ally **Marquis de Lafayette** declared he had never beheld so splendid a man.

Washington's tenacity and firmness of purpose enabled the Continental Army to weather the harsh winters at **Valley Forge** and Morristown, and even to survive the defection of Commander **Benedict Arnold** to the British in 1780. The American commander-in-chief experienced great satisfaction when the American and French armies, supported by the French navy, boxed in General **Charles Cornwallis** at Yorktown and compelled him to surrender.

Washington resigned as commander-in-chief in 1783. He retired briefly to Mount Vernon, but was soon elected the **first president of the United States**. He served two terms, from 1789 to 1797. At the time of his death in 1799, he was perhaps the man most admired in Europe and America. He possessed a rare combination of personal self-control, military audacity, and diplomatic finesse.

63. Nathanael Greene
(1742–1786)

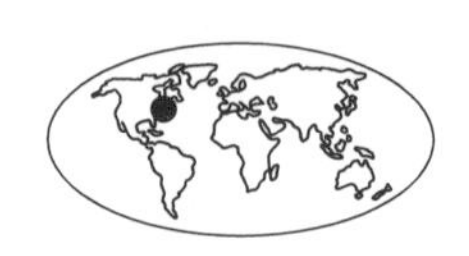

Born in Warwick, Rhode Island, **Nathanael Greene** came from a family of Quakers. He was expelled from the Quakers, who stressed peace, because he held an overweening interest in military studies. When the **Revolutionary War** began in 1775, he was one of the first men named a brigadier general in the **Continental Army**. Greene rose to major-general in 1776.

He went on to serve as quartermaster of the Continental Army (1778–1780). His greatest and most important assignment came in 1780, when **George Washington** (see no. 62) named him commander of the southern forces of the army.

Greene traveled south in the wake of a resounding British victory at Camden, South Carolina. His predecessor, General **Horatio Gates**, had been utterly defeated and the southern forces were in complete disarray at the time of Greene's arrival. To make matters worse, British General **Cornwallis** was about to march into North Carolina and disperse the last remnant of colonial resistance in that state.

Confronted by a nearly impossible situation, Greene disregarded every textbook on warfare. He chose to *divide* his already outnumbered army and march north to the Dan River in two columns. He led one column, and the other was led by General **Daniel Morgan**. Cornwallis pursued Greene while Colonel **Banastre Tarleton** went after Morgan and his men.

Greene's planning paid off handsomely at the **Battle of Cowpens**, where Morgan fought a defensive battle and routed Tarleton. Reeling from this blow, Cornwallis had his men burn their baggage and set off in hot pursuit of Greene. On hearing this news, Greene rejoiced "Then he is ours!" Knowing the speed with which his lightly equipped American troops moved, Greene stayed just out of reach of the British, and crossed the Dan River a few hours prior to the arrival of the British. He took all the boats with him, and Cornwallis could only stare and wonder at the escape of the Americans.

Nathanael Greene

After receiving supplies and reinforcements, Greene again crossed the Dan River and marched to attack Cornwallis. The two armies fought bruising battles at **Hobrik's Hill** and **Guilford Courthouse** (1781). Each time Greene withdrew, leaving Cornwallis in possession of the field with little to show for it but large casualty lists. Explaining his military strategy in a letter, Greene wrote, "We fight, get beat, rise and fight again." No one has better expressed the simple method of guerrilla warfare which Greene employed in the southern campaigns.

By the time the war ended, Greene had chased the British out of all the south except the coastal towns of Charleston and Savannah. His maneuvers forced Cornwallis to march north to Virginia, where he surrendered to George Washington. Greene retired to an estate near Savannah, Georgia. He died soon after the war.

64. Toussaint L'Ouverture
(1743–1803)

Toussaint L'Ouverture was born **Pierre Dominique Toussaint** in the French colony of **St. Dominique**, the western third of the island of **Hispaniola.** (Today, the island is divided between Haiti and the Dominican Republic.) Though he was born and brought up as a slave, L'Ouverture experienced a fairly benevolent upbringing. His master, Bayon de Libertad, educated him in French, Latin, geometry and religion.

Despite this good treatment, L'Ouverture eagerly joined the massive slave revolt that broke out in August 1791 that devastated the sugar plantations of the island. By 1793, L'Ouverture had become the foremost leader of the revolt and was known as "**Father Toussaint**" by his followers. The name "L'Ouverture" (meaning "opening") was given to him at this time; it signified his astute diplomacy in the battles that developed between the slaves, British, French and Spanish troops.

France declared war on both Britain and Spain in 1793. In the warfare that followed, L'Ouverture first joined the Spanish army in **Santo Domingo**. He learned much of his guerrilla warfare tactics from the Spanish. In 1794, when Revolutionary France outlawed the further practice of slavery, L'Ouverture switched sides and joined the French. He soon recaptured much of the area the Spanish had gained. In recognition of his services, L'Ouverture was named brigadier general. He later rose to lieutenant-governor and major general.

After France and Spain made peace in 1795, L'Ouverture fought the British. He forced the surrender of the main body of British troops in 1798. L'Ouverture reached the pinnacle of success in 1800, when peace was declared between France, Britain and Spain. He entered Santo Domingo on January 24, 1801, proclaimed himself "**First of the Blacks**," and with the help of nine compatriots, drafted the first constitution for **Haiti**. L'Ouverture corresponded with First Consul **Napoleon Bonaparte** of the French army (see no. 67), who initially confirmed his position as major general and ruler of the island.

Toussaint L'Ouverture

Napoleon changed his mind in 1802. He dispatched 35,000 French troops and 80 warships to subdue Haiti — the largest expeditionary force France ever sent across the Atlantic.

The French met with disaster in Haiti. The dreaded yellow fever struck and killed at least half the French soldiers within one year. L'Ouverture and the free blacks resisted fiercely. In June 1802, L'Ouverture was abducted during a negotiation. Still wearing the uniform of a French general, L'Ouverture was taken to France on the ship *Heros.* He was brought first to Paris, then to the remote Fort Joux in the Jura mountain range. L'Ouverture's health had already been broken by years of guerrilla warfare, but it seems likely that his spirit was broken by his circumstances and the apparent failure of his people to win their freedom. He died and was buried within the walls of Fort Joux.

L'Ouverture had inspired and led the first truly successful slave revolution in history.

65. Lazare Nicolas Marguerite Carnot (1753–1823)

Lazare Nicolas Marguerite Carnot, the "**Organizer of Victory**" for the French Revolution, became a lieutenant in the French engineering corps in 1774. He rose to captain and joined the Academy of Arras in 1787. There he studied military science and engineering. Having a special interest in fortifications, he devoured the writings of **Sebastien le Prestre de Vauban** (see no. 54).

Lazare Carnot

Carnot became an ardent patriot at the start of the French Revolution. He was elected to the **Legislative Assembly** in 1791 and then to the more radical **National Convention** in 1792. In January 1793, he was one of the delegates who voted to put King **Louis XVI** to death.

Austrian and Prussian forces entered the country and came close to capturing the heart of France during the summer of 1793. Responding to the emergency, the **Committee of Public Safety** was formed. Although it is best known for its indiscriminate use of the **guillotine**, the committee also ran the war effort. Carnot held a prominent place on the committee; by the end of the year he had become the equivalent of both the secretary of defense and minister of propaganda.

Carnot spared no effort to win the war. He called for the ***Levee en masse.*** Issued on August 23, 1793, the new law required all French citizens to contribute to the war effort. By the end of the year, Carnot's troops were winning battles on all fronts. Known as the **Wars of the French Revolution**, Carnot won three of the four major campaigns he waged that year: the **Battle of Hondschoote**, the **Battle of Wattignies** and the **Third Battle of Toulon**. The latter followed defeat at the **Battle of Neerwinden** and lasted from mid-March until mid-December.

They went on the offensive in 1794 and conquered the Netherlands. One of the main reasons for their success was Carnot's strategy. He called for the French army to move in divisions rather than as an entire army. As a result, the French troops traveled more quickly than their foes, and then could concentrate and fight together as one when the situation called for it.

When the Committee of Public Safety fell from power because of its extreme methods, Carnot escaped punishment. He pointed to his record, which demonstrated he had been the indispensable leader needed to save the Revolution from its foreign foes. He served as one of the five directors in the **Directory government** (1795–1799), and then occupied the post of minister of war for **Napoleon** (see no. 67). Carnot quarreled with Napoleon and resigned the position. (Napoleon was the young artillery captain credited for France's victory at Toulon.)

When France was threatened by invasion in 1814, he volunteered to serve and led the defense of the city of **Antwerp**. When Napoleon was finally defeated in 1815, Carnot was exiled from the country because of his status as a regicide ("king killer"). He died in Magdeburg, Prussia, one of the forgotten heroes of Revolutionary France.

66. Horatio Nelson
(1879–1966)

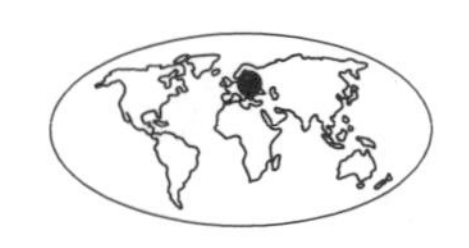

England's greatest naval leader, **Horatio Nelson**, was born at Burnham-Thorpe, in Norfolk. He went to sea as a midshipman at the age of 12 and rose to lieutenant in the Royal Navy by 19. Promoted to post-captain (1779), Nelson served in the Caribbean to enforce the **Navigation Laws** during a time of relative peace (1784–1787).

The start of the French Revolution provided action for Nelson. His first command was that of the 64-gun warship *Agamemnon.* He participated in the capture of the island of **Corsica** (1794) and lost the use of his right eye in combat there.

Nelson had studied and absorbed the lessons of the great 18th-century British commanders Sir George Rooke, Admiral George Anson, Admiral Edward Hawke, and Admiral George Rodney. From them, he created his simple but revolutionary plan of battle: depart from the traditional formation of a line of ships (a formation that had been prevalent for over 100 years) and break the enemy's line. This plan was riskier by far, but it had the potential to win great victories.

Horatio Nelson

This strategy was first evident at the **Battle of Cape Saint Vincent**. Nelson sailed directly into the Spanish line of ships and captured two ships that were both larger than his own. He was knighted and promoted to rear admiral. Nelson went on to meet and completely defeat the French fleet at the **Battle of the Nile** (1798). After this, he was elevated to the level of peer of the realm.

Nelson fought the Danish navy at the **Battle of Copenhagen** (1802). When the battle action was hanging in the balance, he received a signal from his superior officer to retire. Nelson pretended not to see the sign, fought on, and won a complete victory.

His last battle came at **Cape Trafalgar**, off the coast of Spain, in 1805. Nelson had 27 ships; the combined Franco-Spanish fleet had 33 ships including the *Santissima Trinidad,* the largest ship in the world. Nonetheless, the French and Spanish were demoralized from the start, because they knew that Nelson led the British. For his part, Nelson was confident of victory. His last signal to the fleet read "England expects every man will do his duty."

Nelson broke the Franco-Spanish line and battered the enemy with carronades (short-barreled cannons known as "smashers") and double-shotted cannon firing at close quarters. The French and Spanish fought with great courage, but the British gunners were superior. Nelson was wounded on the deck of *HMS Victory* by a bullet from a sharpshooter during the action. He died on board and was brought to St. Paul's Cathedral in London for burial.

67. Napoleon Bonaparte
(1769–1821)

The greatest military genius of modern French history, **Napoleon Bonaparte** was born on the island of **Corsica,** which was conquered by France in the year of his birth. He arrived in France in 1778 to study language and attend a military preparatory school. The onset of the French Revolution provided the opportunity for his keen mind and tremendous will to exert themselves.

Napoleon commanded the artillery that forced the British fleet to evacuate Toulon (1794) and fired cannon shot to disperse the rebellious Parisian crowds in 1795. The new **Directory government** sent him to Italy, where prior commanders had failed to oust the Austrian army. He astounded everyone by defeating the Austrians and their allies. In 1798, he sailed with a large fleet that brought his army to Egypt. He defeated the Mamelukes at the **Battle of the Pyramids,** but then had to return to France after his fleet was destroyed by the British at the **Battle of the Nile.**

Napoleon Bonaparte

Returning to France in 1799, Napoleon overthrew the Directory and set up the new **Consulate government,** with himself as first consul. He soon changed his title to first consul for life, and then to emperor of France in 1804.

Napoleon devised a military system that was both simple and profound. Building on the methods developed by **Lazare Nicolas Marguerite Carnot** during the French Revolution (see no. 65), Napoleon divided the French armies into independent corps that foraged for food, lived off the land, and converged suddenly in the heartland of the enemy. His marshals became brilliant, independent field commanders. Finally, Napoleon used a mass of artillery, infantry and cavalry to break his foe's line at its weakest point.

Napoleon's greatest victories were **Marengo** (1800), **Austerlitz** (1805), **Jena** and **Auerstadt** (1806), and **Friedland** (1807). Even more impressive was the way he snatched victory from defeat by his presence on the battlefield, and the personal impact he had upon the veterans who formed his **Imperial Guard** — the core of the **Napoleonic** armies.

His intervention in Spain and Russia, however, were his downfall. Napoleon's marshals were consistently defeated in Spain by the **Duke of Wellington** (see no. 68). Napoleon personally took 600,000 men into Russia in 1812, but he returned with only 50,000. The fierce Russian defense, grinding battles such as Borodino, and the harsh winter of 1812–1813 all made Napoleon's Russian campaign a terrible disaster.

Napoleon abdicated his throne in 1814 and was exiled to the small island of Elba in the Mediterranean. One year later, he escaped from Elba, returned to France, and became emperor once more, for the brief period of 100 days. He marched north into the Netherlands to meet the British-Prussian armies under the Duke of Wellington. A younger, sharper Napoleon might well have overcome Wellington at **Waterloo,** but the emperor had fought his last battle.

After abdicating a second time, Napoleon was confined by the British to the tiny island of St. Helena in the middle of the Atlantic Ocean. Napoleon died in 1821, the victim of a stomach ailment. Rumors that the British had poisoned him lingered for years.

68. Arthur Wellesley
(1880–1959)

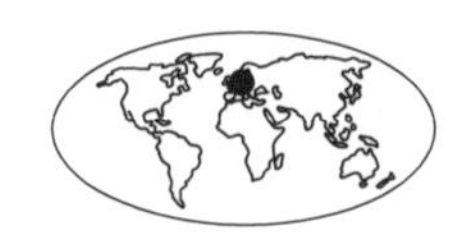

Born in Ireland, **Arthur Wellesley, Duke of Wellington** (known as "Wellington"), joined the British infantry as a lieutenant colonel in 1794. Wellington went with his regiment to India in 1796. There he learned the advantages of knowing the landscape and recruiting allies, which he did among the Indian leaders. He won notable victories at **Assaye** (1803) and **Argaum** (1803). He was then called back to England and given command of a small expeditionary force that landed in Portugal in 1808.

On land, these were the worst of times for the British and their allies. The French emperor, **Napoleon** (see no. 67), had consistently beaten the Austrians, Prussians and Russians, and he had recently placed his brother Joseph on the Spanish throne in Madrid. The success or failure of Wellington's operations therefore assumed a great importance to the British cause.

Perhaps no commander, before or since, has ever understood landscape and topography as clearly as did Wellington. He correctly perceived that the French armies were used to fighting in countries with good road systems and compliant peasant populations. He arranged to have the French cut off from their supply lines and brought many Portuguese over to his side.

The results of Wellington's planning were remarkable. He outmaneuvered and defeated **Massena**, one of the best French marshals, in 1810. He followed with an invasion of French-held Spain and won impressive victories at **Salamanca** (1812) and **Vitoria** (1814). As Napoleon's empire collapsed around him, Wellington invaded France itself and won the **Battle of Toulouse** (1814). After Napoleon escaped from Elba and returned to Paris in 1815, the two most experienced military commanders of their period collided at **Waterloo** on June 18, 1815.

Wellington fought defensively, seeking to hold out until Marshal **Blucher**'s Prussian troops arrived. Positioning his men on a ridge crested by Mount St. Jean, he wore the French down over the course of the day. After Napoleon's **Imperial Guard** made a final, failed assault, Wellington ordered a general charge that soon routed Napoleon's last army. His own comment on the battle was, "It has been a damned nice thing .... By God! I don't think it would have been done if I had not been there."

Wellington later served as a diplomat (1815–1828) and prime minister of Great Britain (1828–1830). His famous nickname, the "**Iron Duke**," referred not to his military capabilities but to the fact that he had iron bars placed over his windows to prevent stones from shattering them during his time as prime minister. Until the time of his death, he was revered as the most astute and far-seeing adviser to Queen **Victoria**.

Sir Arthur Wellesley

69. Karl von Clausewitz
(1780–1831)

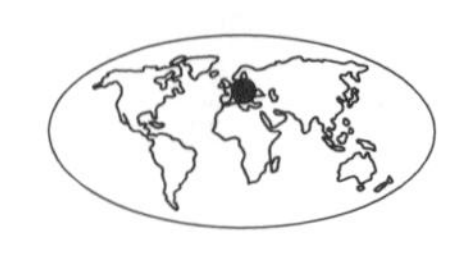

Karl von Clausewitz

Karl von Clausewitz was born in Burg, Prussia, 70 miles from Berlin. His father was a retired Prussian lieutenant. Clausewitz joined the Prussian army at the age of 12 and was made a lance corporal during Prussia's war against Revolutionary France. He rose to the level of subaltern in 1795, and in 1801, he entered the new ***Kriegsakadamie*** (Prussian War Academy) in Berlin.

There he studied military science and philosophy. He thrilled to the theoretical aspects of military studies, but was also drawn to his work by a patriotic desire to see Prussia flourish. When France invaded Prussia under **Napoleon** (see no. 67) in 1806, he volunteered to fight. Clausewitz was captured during the **Battle of Prenzlau** and held prisoner for a year in France, where he observed firsthand the most successful war machine of his day in Napoleon.

After returning to Prussia in 1808, Clausewitz became a major on the Prussian general staff (1810). He also received the post of military tutor to the Crown Prince of Prussia. During this productive time, he also wrote and lectured at the *Kriegsakadamie*.

In 1812, Napoleon invaded Russia. He had taken care to make a treaty with Prussia first, but even so, Clausewitz was outraged at the Corsican's pretensions. He left Prussia, entered Russia, and volunteered for service in the army of Czar **Alexander I.** He served as a staff officer in Russia and was instrumental in the **Treaty of Kalisch** (1813) between Russia and Prussia that brought his home country back into the coalition alliance against Napoleon. During the Waterloo campaign, he served as chief of staff for one of the four Prussian field corps. The **Napoleonic Wars** ended in 1815.

In 1818, Clausewitz was made major general and given the position of director of the *Kriegsakadamie*. There he thrived, writing and lecturing for most of the remainder of his life. His work shaped the careers of many students there, most notably that of **Helmuth von Moltke** (see no. 72).

Clausewitz wrote many tracts, the most important of which was *Vom Kriege* (On War) in 1832. In this seminal work, he surveyed the field of military strategy. Aside from describing military history, he delved into the philosophy of warfare and declared that war was "a mere continuation of policy by other means." In other words, political goals were primary, while military events were secondary.

He discussed the varieties of military tactics and strategies which had evolved during the days of **Sebastien le Prestre de Vauban** (see no. 54). While it was always clear that Clausewitz favored Prussia and the traditions of King **Frederick the Great** (see no. 58), he also took time to examine the contributions made by military innovators such as Napoleon.

Clausewitz returned to active service in 1830. While stationed on the Prussian border with Poland, he contracted cholera and died.

70. Simón Bolívar
(1783–1830)

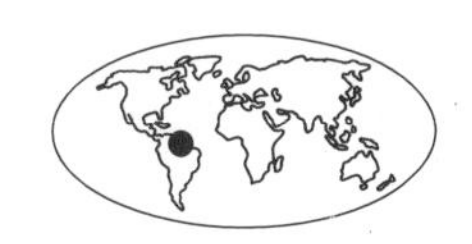

North Americans often refer to **Simón Bolívar** as the "George Washington of South America," for his undying determination to win the freedom of his people from European rule.

Bolívar was born in Caracas, Venezuela, then part of the Spanish empire of South America. A rich Creole by birth, he traveled in Europe. There, he observed the end of the French Revolution and the rise to power of **Napoleon** (see no. 67). Deeply moved by this, on August 15, 1805, Bolívar made a solemn vow in Rome never to rest until he had freed his people from Spanish rule.

Returning home by way of the United States in 1807, Bolívar became the leader of a revolutionary movement that deposed the viceroy of Caracas in 1810 in the fight for Venezuelan independence. Ejected from Caracas, he fled to Cartagena in present-day Colombia. Bolívar led a reconquering of Caracas in 1813, but was forced out by Venezuelan horsemen who supported the royal cause in 1814. Bolívar again went to Cartagena, then to British-held Jamaica, and finally to independent Haiti. In 1816, he launched a seaborne attack on Venezuela that failed.

Simón Bolívar

Truly at the nadir of his fortunes, Bolívar established a base at Angostura on the Orinoco River. He led his men in an epic crossing of the Andes in July 1819 and won the decisive **Battle of Boyaca** on August 7. Soon afterward, he had the satisfaction of seeing Venezuela, **New Granada** (present-day Colombia), and **Quito** (present-day Ecuador) combine into the new **Republic of Gran Colombia.** Bolívar served as the first president.

Continuing the fight against Spanish imperialism, Bolívar won the **Battle of Carabobo** on June 24, 1821. He then traveled to Guayaquil, **Ecuador** in 1822 to meet with **Jose de San Martin**, who had won the war of Chilean independence. The two leaders had a misunderstanding that has never been fully explained. San Martin retired from the scene, and Bolívar and his right-hand lieutenant, **Jose de Sucre**, decided to complete the war for Peruvian independence.

Bolívar had to remain in Gran Colombia during most of the campaign that followed. De Sucre won the crucial battles of **Junin** and **Ayacucho** in 1824 that ended the war.

Bolívar's military actions expelled the Spanish presence from the continent for good. In addition to his military achievements, he wrote the *Cartagena Memorial* (1812) and the *Jamaica Letter* (1815), both of which called for independence from colonialism.

Having attained nearly all of his goals, Bolívar found it impossible to hold together the structure he had created. His "**Great Convention**" of South American states in 1826 was a failure, and in 1830, first Venezuela, and then Quito, seceded from the Republic of Gran Colombia. Bolívar resigned as president of the now-defunct nation and retired in great sadness. Later that same year, he died from tuberculosis.

71. Winfield Scott (1786–1866)

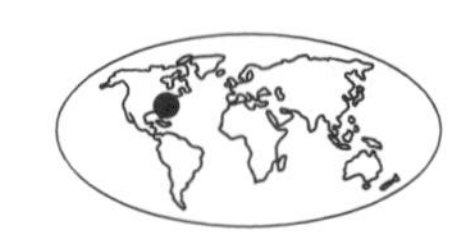

Winfield Scott attended the College of William and Mary and practiced law for a time before turning to military service. He joined the army in 1808. At the beginning of the **War of 1812** , Scott was made a lieutenant colonel.

Given the task of turning raw recruits into true soldiers, Scott marched and drilled his troops under tried and true European methods of discipline. His reward came at the battles of **Chippewa** and **Lundy's Lane** (1814), where his men held their own against the best British regulars, some of whom had served under **Arthur Wellesley, Duke of Wellington** in Spain (see no. 68). Scott ended the war as a brevet major general.

Scott wrote the first set of American army drill regulations, published in 1815. Well-versed in European history, he sought to create an aristocratic officer corps that would be the equal of England's. Scott was made general in chief of the army in 1841 and was promoted to lieutenant general in 1844.

In 1846, Scott received word from President **James Polk** that he would lead the proposed invasion of central Mexico and, if necessary, would prosecute the war all the way to the Mexican capital. Scott took 12,000 troops by ship to Mexico, landed, and besieged the key port city of **Veracruz**. After capturing the city, he made a dangerous decision to advance inland, following almost exactly the invasion route **Hernán Cortéz** had taken in 1521 (see no. 43). Scott's choice to invade quickly was necessitated by the fact that the deadly disease yellow fever would soon hit the coastal lowlands, which happened every summer.

The American army marched into Mexico and won important battles at **Cerro Gordo** on its way to **Mexico City**. Scott and his troops arrived outside the Mexican capital and marveled at both the city and the defenses set up by Mexican general **Santa Anna**. Never daunted, Scott maneuvered to the south and west of the city and won key battles at **Contreras, Churubusco** and **Molino del Reyo**. By September 12, the Americans controlled all the outlying areas, but the fortified citadel of Chapultepec remained.

Winfield Scott

Scott's troops captured **Chapultepec** (Hill of the Grasshoppers) and entered Mexico City itself on September 13; the war was effectively over. Scott served as a model of efficiency in his role as conqueror and administrator; some Mexicans reportedly begged him to serve as their national leader. He returned to the United States (1848) and ran for president on the Whig party ticket in 1852, but was defeated by one of his former military subordinates, Franklin Pierce. Prior to his retirement in 1861, Scott devised the **Anaconda Plan** for strangling the Confederacy through a naval blockade.

72. Helmuth von Moltke
(1800–1891)

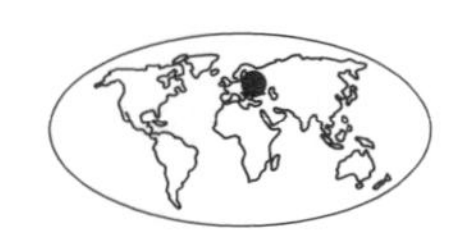

The "Bismarck of the Battlefield," **Helmuth von Moltke,** was born in Parchim, in Mecklenburg, Prussia in 1800. Von Moltke graduated from the royal military academy at Copenhagen and served briefly in the Danish army before joining the Prussian army in 1822. He studied at the *Kriegsakadamie* (Prussian War Academy) and absorbed the lessons offered by **Karl von Clausewitz** (see no. 69), who was the director.

Von Moltke served as a military adviser to the sultan of the Ottoman Empire from 1835 to 1839. He was named first adjutant to Crown Prince **Frederick William** in 1855 and was promoted to major general in 1856. The crucial turning point in his career — and the Prussian army's development — came when he was named chief of the Prussian general staff in 1857.

Having studied the campaigns of **Frederick the Great** of Prussia (see no. 58) and **Napoleon** (see no. 67), von Moltke applied their lessons to the changes brought by new military technology. Planning for future wars, he intended to use the railroad, the telegraph and the industrial production of weapons to achieve a decentralized command structure and a greater concentration of forces at the front. He thereby brought the essence of Napoleonic warfare, mobility, up to date with modern technology. Von Moltke developed Prussia's war machine to strike hard, fast and decisively.

The first test of his tactics came in the **Prussian-Danish War** of 1864. Prussia's solid victory enhanced his stature, and von Moltke prepared for the coming break with Austria. In 1866, Prussia and Austria collided in the **Seven Weeks' War.** Using von Moltke's plans, three large, disconnected Prussian columns of troops entered Austrian territory. They suddenly converged and attacked the shocked Austrians at the **Battle of Koniggratz** which won the war.

By 1870, von Moltke's reputation had grown so formidable that no other Prussian leader would contest his views openly. Rather than attempt to repeat his earlier plans, Von Moltke devised and executed a concentrated attack. His vision worked to perfection; the bulk of the French army, and Emperor **Napoleon III**, surrendered at **Sedan**.

Von Moltke was made a count in 1870 and was promoted to field marshal in 1871, the year the **German Empire** was formed. The creation of the new nation was largely due to the efforts and vision of **Otto von Bismarck** and von Moltke.

In the last years of his life he became distressed by the attitudes of the military clique that surrounded the new Prussian emperor, **Wilhelm II**. He spoke out against the narrow-mindedness of the military leaders at the *Reichstag* (German legislature) in 1890. Von Moltke died while on a visit to Berlin a year later.

Helmuth von Moltke

73. David Farragut
(1801–1870)

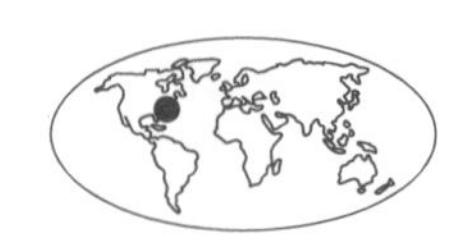

David Farragut was born in Stony Point, Tennessee. His father was **George Farragut**, a Spanish sea captain who fought for the United States in the **Revolutionary War** and settled in Tennessee. After his mother died, the young Farragut was adopted by **David Porter**, a U.S. naval officer who obtained a midshipman's warrant for Farragut in 1810.

Farragut served under Porter on board the *USS Essex* during the **War of 1812**. Farragut was promoted to lieutenant (1825), commander (1841) and captain (1855). He established the **Mare Island Naval Ship Yard** in 1854 (in present-day Vallejo, California).

The start of the **Civil War** gave momentum to his career. When Virginia opted for secession from the Union in April 1861, Farragut immediately moved north and proclaimed himself a Union man. He was named commander of the West Gulf blockading squadron in 1861.

The **Anaconda Plan** designed by General **Winfield Scott** (see no. 71) called for a blockade of the south and a takeover of the Mississippi River. Following orders from Secretary of the Navy **Gideon Welles,** Farragut led 17 wooden ships past the Confederate forts of Jackson and Philip on the lower Mississippi during the night of April 23, 1862. Darkness, fog and smoke helped to keep the casualties low as the Union ships made their way past the forts. Helpless before the guns of Farragut's ships, **New Orleans** surrendered the next day.

Farragut was made rear admiral, the first in the navy's history, and assisted in the capture of **Vicksburg** (1863).

In 1864, he received a mission he had long hungered for — to capture the defenses of Mobile Bay, Alabama. The bay was protected by torpedo mines. The only operable entry channel was protected by the guns of **Fort Morgan**. Farragut took 14 wooden ships and

David Farragut

four ironclad monitors into the channel on August 5, 1864. The leading monitor, the *USS Tecumseh*, hit a mine and sank immediately; the second monitor, the *USS Brooklyn*, began to back its way out of the channel, threatening to pile up the ships behind it. Assessing the situation from aboard the *USS Hartford* (right in line after the *Brooklyn),* Farragut made a famous split-second decision. "Damn the torpedoes," he shouted. "Full speed ahead!"

His ship and the rest of the fleet passed over the mines without incident. Farragut entered the harbor, defeated the Confederate ironclad ship *Tennessee*, and captured all the harbor defenses within the following week. The victory — and his battle cry — made Farragut famous throughout the north.

Promoted to vice admiral (1864) and then to full admiral (1866), Farragut made a goodwill tour of Europe as commander of the Mediterranean fleet from 1867 to 1868. He died while visiting the naval yard at Portsmouth, New Hampshire.

74. Giuseppe Garibaldi
(1807–1882)

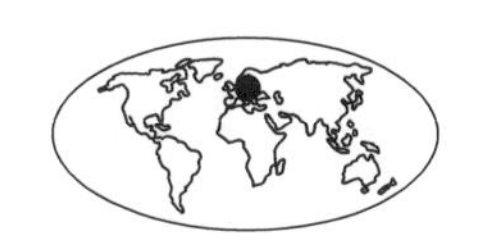

Never before or since has there been a leader who, like **Giuseppe Garibaldi**, stirred the noble and patriotic sentiments of so many people, uniting them in one cause. Born in Nice, France, Garibaldi came from a family of sailors and sea captains. He went to sea in 1822 and became master of his own ship by 1832. Two years later, he embarked on what would become his lifelong cause, the struggle for freedom and Italian unity.

In 1834, Italy consisted of small dukedoms and principalities, most of which were dominated to some extent by Austria. Seeking to change this, Garibaldi joined the revolutionary movement led by **Giuseppe Mazzini.** After the revolt failed, Garibaldi was condemned to death *in absentia* (Latin for "in absence") by the government of Sardinia-Piedmont.

Garibaldi fled to South America. He fought for the state of Rio Grande do Sul against Brazil and for Uruguay in its war with Paraguay.

The turmoil of the European revolutions of 1848 brought Garibaldi back to Italy. He led the troops of Mazzini's Roman Republic and helped Milan fight against Austria. In 1849, he held out heroically in Rome for weeks against the French, Austrian and Neapolitan armies sent against him. Realizing he could no longer hold the Eternal City, he escaped with several thousand of his men in a daring march that caught the imagination of millions of Europeans.

Once again in exile, Garibaldi lived briefly in the United States. Allowed to return to Italy in 1854, he settled on Caprera, a barren island off Sardinia. In 1859, he fought for Sardinia-Piedmont against Austria. On May 6, 1860, he sailed from Genoa with just over 1,000 men, his famous "**Redshirts**." Landing on the island of Sicily, Garibaldi and his men used guerrilla tactics that he had learned in South America to completely outmaneuver and defeat the 25,000-man army of Naples. He crossed the Strait of Messina on September 7 and fought on the Italian mainland, once again driving the enemy forces away through maneuver and deception.

By the fall of 1860, Garibaldi had become the virtual dictator of southern Italy and Sicily. He yielded this, and all claim to a reward, to King **Victor Emmanuel II** of Sardinia-Piedmont, who thereby became king of an Italy that was united except for Venice and Rome itself. Garibaldi then returned to his home island, the hero of millions. He fought to take Venice away from Austria in 1866.

The Italian hero served in his nation's parliament from 1874 to 1876, where he found his liberal ideas constantly on the fringes. He was strongly anti-clerical and mildly socialist and believed in both racial and sexual equality. Garibaldi died at Caprera in 1882.

Giuseppe Garibaldi

75. Robert E. Lee
(1807–1870)

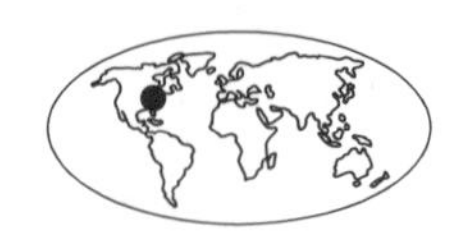

Robert E. Lee was born at his family estate of Stratford in Westmoreland County, Virginia. His father was **Henry "Light-Horse Harry" Lee,** a well-known **Revolutionary War** soldier. Lee graduated second in his class from **U.S. Military Academy at West Point.**

Glory first came to Lee during his service in the **Mexican War.** Serving as a scout, an engineer and a builder of bridges, he made the American march from Veracruz to Mexico City possible. He received the highest possible commendation from General **Winfield Scott** (see no. 71) for his services.

The start of the **Civil War** found Lee in personal conflict. He believed in the Union and was in fact offered the supreme command of the U.S. armies by President **Abraham Lincoln's** chief of staff, Winfield Scott. After his home state of Virginia seceded from the Union on April 17, 1861, however, he resigned his commission and joined the **Confederate** army.

Lee became a full general in the Confederate armies, and at the end of May 1862, he replaced General Joe Johnston as commander of the Army of Northern Virginia. In his new capacity, Lee immediately showed the breathtaking audacity that would become his trademark. He attacked a Union contingent that outnumbered his own by two-to-one and drove it back during the **Battle of Seven Days.** Lee's actions saved Richmond.

Using his quiet charisma, personal daring, and the services of talented subordinates such as **Thomas "Stonewall" Jackson** (see no. 78), Lee won impressive victories at the **Second Battle of Bull Run** (1862), **Fredericksburg** (1862) and **Chancellorsville** (1863).

Knowing that he needed to win a victory on northern soil, Lee pushed north twice. He was fought to a standstill at **Antietam** (1862). In June 1863, he moved north again and collided with the Union armies at **Gettysburg,** Pennsylvania. Confident that his men would follow him anywhere and carry the day, Lee sent them forward on the disastrous attack known as **Pickett's Charge.** Seven thousand men were lost in a half-hour, men whom the South could not replace.

Robert E. Lee

After Gettysburg, Lee was permanently on the defensive. He fought a grinding set of battles against General **Ulysses S. Grant** (see no. 76). However, the high Union casualties at The Wilderness, Spotsylvania Court House and Cold Harbor did not dissuade Grant. Lee was soon surrounded and besieged in a 20-mile ring from Richmond to Petersburg. In this confined setting, Lee's tactical brilliance had little effect.

Lee and his men broke out from the siege in the spring of 1865 but were quickly run down by the Union armies. Lee surrendered to Grant at the **Appomattox Courthouse** on April 9, effectively ending the war. Paroled on his honor, Lee later served as president of Washington College in Virginia.

76. Ulysses S. Grant
(1822–1885)

Ulysses S. Grant was born in Point Pleasant, Ohio. His early schooling was limited, but his fine horsemanship helped him win entrance to the **U.S. Military Academy at West Point**. He graduated and was commissioned a lieutenant.

When the **Civil War** began, Grant became a brigadier general of volunteers in 1861. He showed both strategic brilliance and personal resolve by capturing Confederate forts **Donelson** and **Henry** (1862), thereby opening Tennessee to Union forces. This, the first major Union victory of the Civil War, catapulted "Unconditional Surrender" Grant to national recognition.

That same year, Grant went on to fight the Confederates to a standstill at **Shiloh**, and he led a remarkable campaign to capture the Confederate fortress of **Vicksburg**, located on the eastern side of the Mississippi River. The surrender of Vicksburg on July 4, 1863, brought about great rejoicing in the north. Grant was promoted to major-general of the army, and then was elevated to the post of general of all the Union armies in March 1864.

In the spring of 1864, Grant marched south from Washington, D.C., seeking to capture the Confederate capital of Richmond, Virginia. He fought a set of grueling battles against General **Robert E. Lee** (see no. 75) at The Wilderness, Spotsylvania Court House and Cold Harbor. Having lost 17,666 men, Grant continued to press southward, leading news reporters in the North to call him "Butcher Grant." Knowing he had the confidence of President **Abraham Lincoln**, Grant continued to apply vise-like pressure to the Confederate Army of Northern Virginia.

Grant besieged Lee in a circle around the cities of Richmond and Petersburg for 10 months (June 1864–April 1865). When Lee escaped from Richmond, Grant pursued him relentlessly. Lee finally surrendered to Grant at the **Appomattox Courthouse**, ending the war. Grant gave generous terms to the Confederates and returned home the hero of the war.

His military success led to political success. Grant ran for and easily won the White House for two terms. As U.S. president from 1869 to 1877, he often lacked the diplomacy and subtlety required for the position. He also was deceived by many of his political favorites, who indulged themselves in corruption and scandal.

After his second term ended, Grant fell on such hard economic times that he actually sold his swords and souvenirs from the Civil War. Learning he had throat cancer, Grant rushed to write his *Personal Memoirs,* published posthumously by **Mark Twain**. Grant finished the book just in time; it earned over $400,000 in royalties, providing for his family after his death.

Ulysses S. Grant

77. William T. Sherman
(1822–1891)

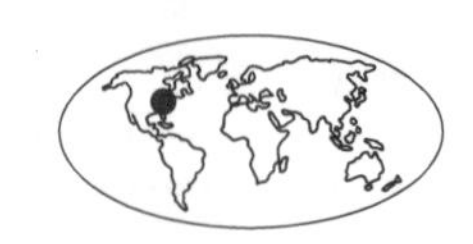

William Tecumseh Sherman was born in Lancaster, Ohio. His birth father had named him "Tecumseh" in honor of the Indian chief, but his foster parents later gave him the first name William. Sherman went to the **U.S. Military Academy at West Point** and graduated sixth in his class of 42. Commissioned a lieutenant of artillery, he served at Fort Moultrie in the harbor of Charleston, South Carolina.

Sherman saw no active service during the Mexican War. Bored by peacetime army life, he resigned his commission in 1853 and worked briefly as both a banker and a lawyer. From 1859 to 1861, Sherman was superintendent of a military academy in Louisiana.

At the start of the **Civil War**, Sherman was commissioned a colonel and led a brigade at the **First Battle of Bull Run** (1861). Sherman became a devoted friend of General **Ulysses S. Grant** (see no. 76), and he planned Grant's campaign against forts Henry and Donelson in 1862. Sherman went on to play a major role in Grant's campaign against **Vicksburg** in 1863. When Grant was named lieutenant general of all the Union Armies in 1864, Sherman succeeded his friend as commander of the forces in the West. The two planned a simple campaign, Grant would drive south against **Robert E. Lee** (see no. 75) and capture Richmond, while Sherman would drive east against General **Joe Johnston** and seize Atlanta.

Sherman executed a brilliant campaign. He captured Atlanta on September 2, 1864, through a series of intricate maneuvers rather than head-on fighting. He then decided on a brutal approach to end the war. Sherman telegraphed Grant on October 9, 1864, saying, "I can make the march, and make Georgia howl." He was true to his word. Sherman led 60,000 men in a broad, 50-mile wide swath southeast to the sea, burning or destroying everything of value in sight. This infamous "**March to the Sea**" (November 16–December 22, 1864) ended with Sherman in Savannah. He then marched north and, as the Confederacy crumbled, accepted the surrender of General Johnston near Durham, North Carolina on April 26, 1865.

William T. Sherman

Sherman rose to lieutenant general (1866), then full general (1869), and served as general in chief of the army (1869–1883). He retired and went to live in St. Louis and then New York City. He vigorously refused a Republican nomination for president in 1884. A complex man, Sherman is remembered for his high temper, generous nature and famous statement that "war is hell," which he made to the graduating class of the Michigan Military Academy in 1879.

78. Thomas "Stonewall" Jackson
(1824–1863)

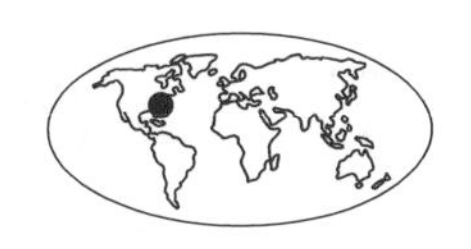

Both in his lifetime and afterward, **Thomas Jonathan "Stonewall" Jackson** had been a source of pride and the making of a myth. He was born in Clarksburg, Virginia, in what is now West Virginia. He received little early education and was fortunate to be admitted to the **U.S. Military Academy at West Point** when space opened up after another applicant declined to enter. He graduated in 1846 and immediately entered the **Mexican War** as a second lieutenant.

Jackson served in all the important battles from Veracruz to Mexico City in 1847. Returning to the United States, he resigned his commission in 1851 after an altercation with his superior officer at Fort Meade, Florida. Jackson obtained a position teaching philosophy and military tactics at the **Virginia Military Institute.**

During the **Civil War,** Jackson remained a firm believer in the Union until Virginia seceded on April 17, 1861. He then cast his lot with the Confederacy and became a colonel of the Virginia state forces. At the **First Battle of Bull Run,** Confederate General **Bernard E. Bee** rallied his men at a critical moment by pointing to Jackson's fortitude on the battlefield and crying out, "There is Jackson, standing like a stone wall! Let us determine to die here, and we will conquer." The nickname "Stonewall" Jackson stuck, but the irony was that Jackson became far better known for the lightning speed of his maneuvers than for standing fast in position.

"Stonewall" Jackson

Promoted to the rank of Confederate major general, Jackson created the "**Stonewall Brigade.**" Between April and June of 1862, he won a remarkable string of victories in his famous **Shenandoah Valley** campaign. Jackson defeated General **Robert Milroy** on May 8, General **Nathaniel Banks** on May 23 and 25, General **John C. Fremont** on June 8, and General **Thomas Shields** on June 9. These victories drew 60,000 troops into the Shenandoah Valley region and relieved the pressure on the Confederate capital of Richmond that spring.

Jackson was instrumental in the Confederate victory at the **Second Battle of Bull Run.** He captured **Harper's Ferry** in September 1862. Promoted to lieutenant general, he took part in the defensive victory at **Fredericksburg** (1862).

The **Battle of Chancellorsville** in May 1863 was Jackson's and **Robert E. Lee**'s masterpiece (see no. 75). Outnumbered two-to-one by Union general **Joseph Hooker,** Lee held Hooker at bay with a mere shadow force while Jackson swooped around Hooker's right flank and hit him with a devastating counterattack. The Union flank reeled, and the Confederates were on their way to a decisive victory when Jackson was hit by bullets from his own troops. They had mistaken him for a Union officer as he rode back to his own lines. His left arm shattered, Jackson sought to recuperate, but pneumonia set in and he died on May 10, 1863.

79. Geronimo (1829–1909)

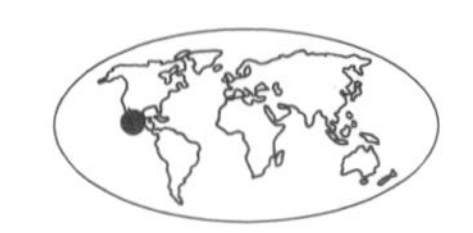

His Indian name was **Goyathlay**, meaning, "He who yawns." **Geronimo** was born in No-Doyohn Canyon, Mexico in 1829. His people, the **Chiricahua Apache**, had a long tradition of fighting Spanish and, then, Mexican troops from the south.

Geronimo was admitted to his tribe's **Council of Warriors** in 1846. The turning point in his life came in 1851 when his mother, wife and children were killed in a Mexican surprise attack near Janos, Chihuahua. Swearing eternal vengeance, Geronimo led a number of raids into Mexico. The ferocity of his attacks caused the Mexicans to call upon St. Jerome for protection. Their utterances of "Jerome, Jerome" led to the Indian warrior's name "Geronimo."

Meanwhile, American settlers had encroached on Apache land from the north and east. In 1871, a reservation was established in eastern Arizona for the Apache nation. Finding himself confined to a small locality, Geronimo broke the peace. In 1874, he and the majority of his people were moved to the **San Carlos Reservation** on the Gila River in east-central Arizona. The Apaches detested this barren wasteland, and Geronimo led guerrilla attacks against American settlements in the territory. Hundreds of Apaches chose to leave the reservation with him and conduct a war against the Americans.

Geronimo surrendered to American general **George Crook** in January 1884. After being returned to the San Carlos reservation, he fled with 35 men, eight boys and 101 women in May 1885. Again he conducted raids against both American and Mexican settlements. He was finally cornered by General Crook and surrendered at **Canon de Los Embudos** in Sonora, Mexico on March 27, 1886. As the Americans conducted their prisoners on a march to the United States, Geronimo and a few others bolted as they neared the U.S. border. As a result of this escape, General Crook was replaced by General **Nelson Miles**.

Geronimo

Miles led 5,000 U.S. soldiers and some 500 Indian auxiliary troops in a year-long search for Geronimo. The Americans finally tracked the Apache leader to his camp in the Sonora mountains. There, Miles persuaded Geronimo to surrender on September 3, 1886, with a promise that he would eventually be allowed to return to his Arizona homeland.

The pledge was broken. Geronimo and his fellow warriors were taken to Florida and forced to do hard labor. They were transferred to Fort Sill in the Oklahoma Territory in 1894. Geronimo dictated his autobiography before he died of pneumonia in 1909. He had never been allowed to return to Arizona.

80. Chief Joseph
(1832–1904)

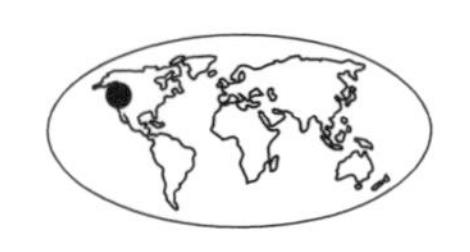

Born in the Wallowa Valley of present-day Washington state, **Chief Joseph**'s Native American name was **Hinmaton Yalaktit** ("Thunder Rolling in the Heights"). The son of a **Nez Percé** (NAY-per-SAY) Indian chief, he became a chief after his father died around 1862.

American settlers flocked to the Pacific Northwest region in the 1840s and 1850s. In 1863, the U.S. government negotiated a treaty that confined the Nez Percé to the **Lapwai Reservation** in Idaho, removing them from their lands near the shores of the Pacific Ocean. From that day forward, the Nez Percé were divided into two groups: the "treaty" and "non-treaty."

Chief Joseph became the leader of the "non-treaty" population which refused to be confined to any reservation area.

U.S. General **Oliver Howard** went to parley with the Nez Percé at the council at Fort Lapwai in the spring of 1877. He and Joseph commenced negotiations when a small band of Nez Percé murdered four white settlers. The negotiations ended, and the **Nez Percé War** began, despite the best efforts of Howard and the chief.

Joseph led his band of 300 warriors to a victory at **White Bird Canyon**. Far from exultant over the win, Joseph persuaded his fellow chiefs to begin a march to elude the U.S. troops and reach the safety of Canada. He led approximately 750 men, women and children in a grueling march over the Rocky Mountains and across the Missouri River, seeking the safety of "Grandmother Victoria's," Canada — the land ruled by Queen Victoria of England.

Along the march, Joseph defeated General **John Gibbon** at the **Battle of Big Hole** (Wisdom River, Montana) and also won encounters such as the Cottonwood skirmish and the **Battle of Canyon Creek**. By late September, Joseph and his people reached the Bear Paw Mountains in Montana, a mere 40 miles south of the Canadian border.

Unbeknownst to Joseph, another U.S. cavalry group had entered Montana from the East. General **Nelson A. Miles** and 350 troopers found the Nez Percé and attacked them. Joseph arranged his men in trenches so cleverly that they foiled all attacks, but the Nez Percé had been stopped. More U.S. soldiers arrived over the next five days, and on October 5, 1877, Chief Joseph made his surrender.

A total of 431 Nez Percé were taken as prisoners to **Fort Leavenworth** in Kansas, including 87 Indian warriors. A well-known figure in his later years, Joseph survived his time in prison and he sent numerous petitions to Washington, D.C. asking to return to his tribal homeland. They were refused. He died at Nespelim on the **Colville Reservation** in Washington.

Chief Joseph

81. Paul von Hindenburg
(1847–1934)

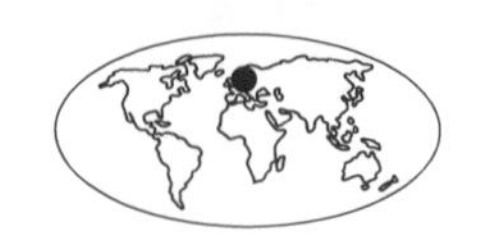

Born in Posen, Prussia (present-day Poznan, Poland), **Paul von Hindenburg**'s family traced its German roots to the era of the **Teutonic Knights**. Von Hindenburg entered the Prussian cadet corps in 1858 and fought as a lieutenant at the important **Battle of Sadowa** against Austria in 1866. He won the Iron Cross for bravery in the **Franco-Prussian War** and represented his regiment at the signing of the **Treaty of Versailles** (1871).

Elevated to the Prussian general staff in 1878, von Hindenburg served with merit. In 1903 he was promoted to lieutenant general. Von Hindenburg retired from the army in 1911 and went to Hanover.

When **World War I** began in 1914, Von Hindenburg asked for and received an important field command, defending East Prussia against the invasion of two Russian armies. Von Hindenburg teamed up with **Erich von Ludendorff**, his chief of staff. The two were a remarkable military duo. Von Hindenburg was cautious and methodical; Ludendorff was lightning-quick and sometimes rash. The two men masterminded brilliant victories over the Russians at her and the Masurian Lakes.

By 1915, von Hindenburg was a field marshal and commander-in-chief on the German eastern front. He won another impressive victory at Lodz, and in August 1916, he replaced **Erich von Falkenhayn** as chief of the Prussian General Staff. Von Hindenburg and Ludendorff joined forces again and took over the war effort. Kaiser **Wilhelm II** became something of a figurehead as the two military men masterminded Germany's moves from 1916 to 1918.

The two soldiers made at least one clear blunder, their decision to use unrestricted submarine warfare caused the United States to join the Allies against Germany. When the tide went against Germany in 1918, Ludendorff resigned, leaving von Hindenburg in authority. The field marshal presided quietly over the end of the war in 1919 and retired to his estate, still highly regarded by the German people.

Paul von Hindenburg (*left*)

In 1925, he accepted an effort to draft his services and ran for president of the **Weimar Republic**. He was elected and served as a moderate and judicious head of state from 1926 to 1934.

Von Hindenburg met the final challenge of his life — Adolf Hitler — when he was too old to shape events. The Nazi leader ran against von Hindenburg in the 1932 presidential elections. Even though von Hindenburg won, he had to accept Hitler as chancellor of the Reich in January 1933.

Hitler ran the nation during the last year of von Hindenburg's life. He used von Hindenburg's name and reputation to lend credence to the Nazi movement, acting as if the old Prussian values espoused by men such as von Hindenburg stood behind the Nazi regime. In fact they did not, but von Hindenburg was unable to demonstrate this prior to his death in 1934.

82. Heihachiro Togo
(1848–1934)

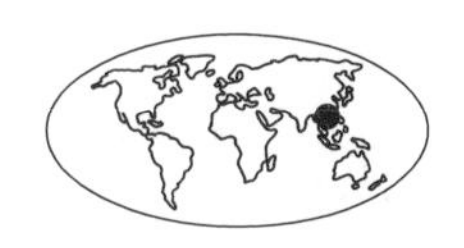

The greatest Japanese naval leader of modern times was born in Kajima-Machi in Kyushu, Japan. Raised amidst the turmoil created by American commodore **Oliver H. Perry**'s "opening up" of Japan to the West, **Heihachiro Togo** joined the Satsuma provincial navy in 1866. Four years later, he entered the new imperial Japanese navy as a cadet and went to England for seven years of training in naval tactics (1871–1878). He greatly admired Admiral **Horatio Nelson** (see no. 66) and made it a point to travel to Cape Trafalgar to see the site of his hero's greatest victory.

Togo supervised the building of the *Yamoto,* one of Japan's first modern warships, and served as its first commander. In 1890, he created an international stir by firing upon and sinking a British steamer during the start of the **Japanese-Chinese War** in 1894. It was found that the British ship was carrying Chinese troops, and Togo was therefore not reprimanded for his action.

Togo headed the Advanced Naval College and was made commander of the new naval base at Sasebo in 1899. In 1900, he observed the Russian ships during the police actions of the **Boxer Rebellion** in China and concluded they were less efficient than was generally believed. When war between Russia and Japan became imminent in 1903, Togo was made commander-in-chief of the **Imperial Navy**, flying his flag aboard the ship *Mikasa.*

Following orders from his high command, Togo fired the first shots of the **Russo-Japanese War**, sending torpedo boats into the harbor of Port Arthur to attack the Russian ships there on February 6, 1904. Foreshadowing Pearl Harbor, this sneak attack gave the initiative to the Japanese, who never relinquished it during the war. Togo's naval blockade of Port Arthur and Vladivostok secured Japanese communications between their home islands and the war in Korea and Manchuria.

Togo's greatest triumph came August 27 and 28, 1905, at the **Battle of Tshushima Straits**. A large Russian fleet had sailed from the Baltic Sea to the Sea of Japan. The smaller but better-armed Japanese fleet completely outmaneuvered and defeated the Russians. Togo lost only 117 men and three torpedo boats, while killing 4,830 enemy soldiers and capturing the entire Russian fleet.

The hero of the war, Togo was made a count (1907), then a marquis (1934), and was given the special title of admiral of the fleet (1913). He did not serve in World War I, but the men who did had been his pupils. Made a permanent member of the Imperial General Staff, Togo remained one of the most revered leaders in Japan until his death in 1934. He was the first Japanese man not of the royal lineage to be honored with a national funeral.

Heihachiro Togo

83. Ferdinand Foch
(1851–1929)

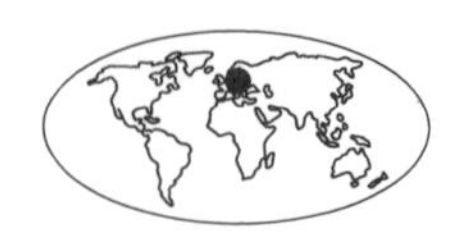

Known for his audacity and belief in a relentless offense, **Ferdinand Foch**, born in Tarbes, Hautes-Pyrenees, France, studied at the Ecole Polytechnique and became a lieutenant of artillery in 1873. Foch believed in the rules of war established by **Napoleon** (see no. 67), but he failed to appreciate the difference that machine gun and trench warfare would make on the battlefield in the future.

Foch was already a general when **World War I** began. He led his men in an inspired defense of the St. Gond area during the critical **Battle of the Marne** (September 6–9, 1914). During the "**Race to the Sea**" that followed the Marne, Foch won the attention and admiration of General **Joseph Joffre** of France, who became his patron. Joffre sent Foch north to coordinate movements of the French, British and Belgian armies, no small task given their differences in language and temperament.

Foch commanded the northern army group during 1915 and 1916. He was criticized by his allies for his troop allotments during the German gas attack at **Ypres**, and he failed to make any noticeable gains during the Somme campaign (1916). The lowest point of his career came when Joffre was removed from overall command, but Foch bounced back to prominence when Joffre's replacement was himself replaced by General **Henri Pétain** (see no. 84). Foch became chief of the general staff in 1917.

Germany made an enormous effort to break the deadlock early in 1918. During a collapse in the allied line, French and British leaders agreed to name Foch "generalissimo" of the combined forces. Belgium and the United States followed suit, making Foch the supreme allied commander for the rest of the war.

The German attacks faltered in June, and by July, Foch was on the offensive everywhere.

Ferdinand Foch

He disagreed frequently with General **John Pershing** of the United States. Foch wanted to establish his dominance in the relationship, but had to accept the fact that the two million American soldiers were essential to the war effort. Foch planned and coordinated the tremendous allied offensives that broke the **Siegfried Line** on the German border and brought the German diplomats to the peace table. Foch himself dictated the terms of the armistice to the Germans in a railway car at **Compiegne** on November 11, 1918. It was sweet satisfaction for the man who had witnessed his nation's defeat in the **Franco-Prussian War** 48 years earlier.

Foch was disappointed by the **Treaty of Versailles**; he believed it was too soft on the Germans. He made a tour of the United States in 1921, and received numerous honors from various countries prior to his death.

84. Henri Phillipe Pétain
(1856–1951)

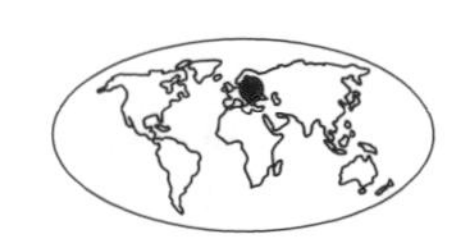

First a great hero, then a tragic collaborator, **Henri Pétain** came to symbolize much of what was noble and perverse in France during the two world wars.

He graduated from the military academy at St. Cyr in 1887. The French army was demoralized by its defeat in the **Franco-Prussian War** of 1870. French people wanted revenge, and military thinking at the time emphasized a vigorous offense by infantrymen. Pétain disagreed with this notion, which was one reason he had risen only to colonel by the time **World War I** began in 1914.

French offensives stumbled badly in 1914, and, as a new emphasis on careful planning and defensive fighting gained favor, Pétain rose in leadership. He became a full general in 1916 and then commander of the Second Army. In February 1916, Pétain was named commander of the French forces defending the fortress of **Verdun** against the Germans. Pétain told his troops, "*Ils ne passeront pas*" ("They shall not pass"), and he was good as his word. Both sides suffered tremendous human losses during the six-month battle, but the French held their positions.

In May 1917, Pétain became commander-in-chief of the French army. He was passed over by General **Ferdinand Foch** (see no. 83) for supreme allied commander in 1918, but he remained in charge of the French army until the end of the war.

A hero to his countrymen, Pétain served briefly as a minister of war, and then as an ambassador to Spain between World War I and **World War II**. He urged the construction of the **Maginot Line** to defend France (the line was never completed, leaving France vulnerable to a flanking attack through Belgium).

In May 1940, Adolf Hitler's forces struck at France. The speed of their offense (especially their tanks) won the battle over France within one month. Pétain came out of retirement and was named premier of France on June 16. Rather than urge a fight to the death or flee to an allied country, Pétain signed an armistice, and then a peace treaty, with the Germans. He was allowed to govern the unoccupied zone of France.

Pétain earned the contempt, and even hatred, of many people during his time as chief of the **Vichy government** (1940–1944). He urged his countrymen to quietly endure the Nazi occupation at a time when many French people yearned to join the **Resistance movement**. Pétain and his fellow collaborators helped the Germans find labor conscripts in France, and thousands of French Jews were turned over to the Nazis.

After the Allies won World War II, Pétain was tried, convicted and sentenced to death. President **Charles De Gaulle** commuted the sentence to life imprisonment.

Henri Phillipe Pétain

85. John Pershing
(1860–1948)

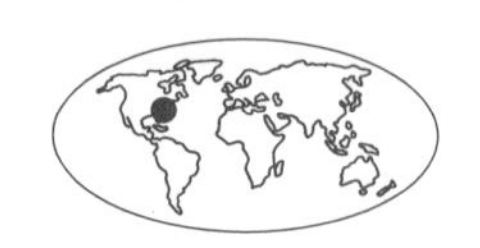

America's military leader in World War I came from the prairie hamlet of Laclede, Missouri. **John Pershing** worked on his father's farm and taught at a country school while still in his teens. He went to the **U.S. Military Academy at West Point** and graduated as senior cadet captain in 1886.

Pershing became a cavalry lieutenant. He fought against **Geronimo** (see no. 79) of the Apache nation as well as the Sioux nation during his early military years. He then taught military tactics at the University of Nebraska (1893–1897). Pershing demonstrated his valor in the **Spanish-American War** and won a Silver Star for gallantry in combat.

Pershing served in the Philippines (1901–1903) and as America's official observer during the Russo-Japanese War (1904–1905). Deeply impressed by Pershing's reports, President **Theodore Roosevelt** promoted him from captain to brigadier general in 1906, bypassing 862 senior officers. Pershing served three more years in the Philippines and then was sent to the Mexican border in 1915.

He pursued the Mexican revolutionary **Francisco "Pancho" Villa** into Mexican territory. Returning from the foray, Pershing was named commander of the **American Expeditionary Force**, which was to be created and sent to the European battlefields in **World War I.**

Pershing arrived in France in June 1917. His presence allowed **Charles E. Stanton** to visit the grave of the Marquis de Lafayette and declare, "Lafayette, we are here," on July 4, 1917. Determined to keep American troops together as a separate army, Pershing clashed loudly and often with both British and French leaders. Their calls for him to be replaced went unheeded; the grim, effective American remained as the leader of his nation's forces in Europe.

John Pershing

Made a full general in 1917, Pershing oversaw the creation and deployment of a two-million-person U.S. Army. His men won the crucial battles of **Belleau Wood** and **Chateau Thierry**, stopping the last German offensive. Pershing coordinated a huge American offensive in the **Meuse-Argonne** area in the last weeks of the war.

Named general of the armies in 1919, Pershing returned home to tremendous praise from the American public and government. He hoped to be asked to run for the presidency in 1920 but was not, so he retired from the army in 1924, and served as chairperson of the **Battle Monuments Commission** for the rest of his life. Pershing died in Washington, D.C. and was buried at Arlington National Cemetery.

86. Bernard Montgomery
(1887–1976)

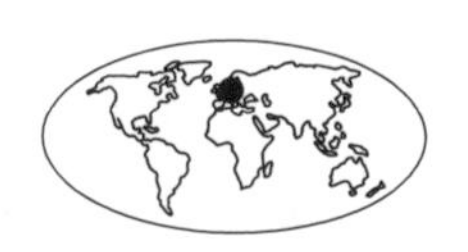

Known as "Monty" to his soldiers, **Bernard Law Montgomery** compiled a long list of accomplishments during half a century in the British army. Montgomery graduated from the **Royal Military Academy** in 1908 and was commissioned as an infantry lieutenant. He served in France and Belgium during **World War I** and received the Distinguished Service Order after he was wounded.

Montgomery rose to major general and was in command of a division in British-held Palestine at the start of **World War II**. He was immediately transferred to France, where he evacuated the Third Division out of Dunkirk in 1940. He began a program of intensive training for his men, aimed at turning them into troops that could meet and defeat their German counterparts.

In August 1942, Prime Minister **Winston Churchill** selected Montgomery to take command of the British troops in Africa. Taking charge after Britain's loss of Tobruk to General **Erwin Rommel** of Germany (see no. 94), Montgomery remained on the defensive at first. He built up a formidable strike force in Egypt. After Rommel's attacks failed to penetrate the British perimeter, Montgomery went on the offensive. The resulting **Battle of El Alamein** (October 1942) was the first major loss in the field inflicted on the Germans during the war. Montgomery's meticulous preparation and execution in North Africa earned him a knighthood and promotion to full general.

Montgomery led the British troops in the Allied invasion of **Sicily** in 1943. He was selected as the ground commander of the European invasion force, but the position of supreme commander went to General **Dwight D. Eisenhower** of the U.S.

The British, American, Canadian and Australian units that landed in Normandy on **D-Day**, June 6, 1944, made slow progress at first. Feelings of resentment grew between Montgomery and some of the allied commanders, notably General **George Patton** of the U.S. (see no. 91). Montgomery's planning went awry at the **Battle of Arnhem** in September, where 6,000 airborne troops were lost. Having been criticized for this, Montgomery spared no opportunity to chastise the Americans for their initial defeats in the **Battle of the Bulge** (December 1944).

Montgomery was raised to field marshal (1944) and when the war ended he became chief of the Imperial General Staff. He later served as deputy to Eisenhower at the **North Atlantic Treaty Organization** (NATO). What had begun as a friendly rivalry between the two men escalated over the years into a bitter invective, as each lambasted the other in his memoirs of the war years. Certainly the greatest British general of the 20th century, Montgomery lacked the tact and subtlety for positions that required close coordination with allied forces.

Bernard Montgomery

87. Douglas MacArthur (1880–1964)

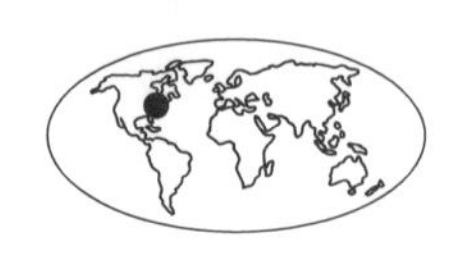

Douglas MacArthur was born in an army barracks in Little Rock, Arkansas. His father was a general, and MacArthur never considered any career other than the military. He graduated first in his class at the **U.S. Military Academy at West Point** in 1903 and entered the army corps of engineers. A major when **World War I** began, he led the famous **42nd "Rainbow" Division** and was twice wounded. Promoted to brigadier general by the end of the war, he then served as the youngest superintendent ever of West Point (1919–1923).

Douglas MacArthur

MacArthur's life and career were inextricably intertwined with the **Philippine Islands**, where his father had served before him. MacArthur came to love the islands during a tour of duty there in the 1920s. He then served as chief of staff of the U.S. Army. He officially retired from the army in 1937 and went to the Philippines as a military adviser.

The start of **World War II** saw MacArthur back on active duty on the islands. His air force was stricken by the Japanese only hours after the attack on **Pearl Harbor** (December 7, 1941). After a futile effort to defend the archipelago, he left, vowing "I shall return."

MacArthur became supreme commander of the southwest Pacific ground forces in April 1942. After taking steps to protect Australia from invasion, he led U.S. troops in the "island hopping" campaigns that brought him back to the Philippines in 1944 as promised. Had the war continued after the use of the atomic bomb, he would have led **Operation Downfall**, the projected invasion of the Japanese mainland. Lacking that, he had the satisfaction of accepting the Japanese surrender aboard the *USS Missouri* (September 2, 1945).

As supreme commander of the Allied occupation of Japan from 1945 to 1951, MacArthur held vast power, which he used with judgment and skill. He established a liberal democracy, abolished the nobility, and revived Japanese industry, starting the recovery process that would make Japan into an economic superpower by the 1980s.

When the **Korean War** broke out, MacArthur was given command of the American and **United Nations** forces defending **South Korea**. He planned and executed a brilliant and daring amphibious landing at **Inchon** behind the lines of the North Korean troops. His movement led to a wholesale rout. MacArthur vowed to chase the North Koreans into China itself.

His belief in final victory proved premature. China intervened in the war and hurled the Americans back southward. MacArthur called on President **Harry Truman** to use nuclear weapons if necessary; Truman refused. After MacArthur proceeded to make his feelings about the war public, Truman removed him from command on April 11, 1951. MacArthur then returned to the United States, which he had not seen since the start of World War II.

88. William Halsey, Jr.
(1882–1959)

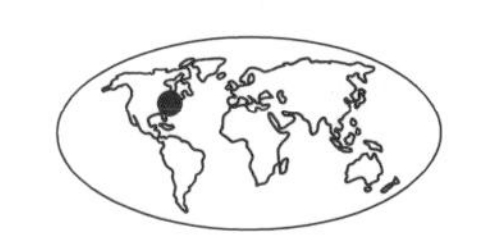

William "Bull" Halsey, Jr. led the U.S. Navy in many of the most important battles of World War II. Halsey was the son of a naval officer. He graduated from the **U.S. Naval Academy at Annapolis** (1904) and sailed aboard the "**Great White Fleet**" as a midshipman.

Halsey commanded destroyers in convoy escort duty across the North Atlantic in **World War I** and was awarded the Navy Cross. After becoming a specialist in torpedo warfare, he commanded groups of destroyers, and then groups of aircraft carriers during the 1920s and 1930s. Finding part of his vocation late in life, he attended flight school and earned the wings of a naval aviator at the age of 52.

When **World War II** began, Halsey was a vice-admiral in command of the aircraft carrier *USS Enterprise.* Away from **Pearl Harbor**, he escaped the Japanese attack of December 7, 1941. Not content to defend in the Pacific, he attacked the Japanese at **Wake Island** early in 1942. Even more important for American morale, he brought the *USS Hornet* within 800 miles of Japan. Lieutenant Colonel **James Doolittle** launched his B-25 bombers from the aircraft carrier's deck and led the first aerial bombing of Tokyo on April 18, 1942. As Americans rallied from the destruction of Pearl Harbor, Halsey became a household word; newspapers began to call him "Bull."

In October 1942, Halsey was named commander of the South Pacific Force and promoted to full admiral that November. He defeated the Japanese in key naval battles off the island of **Guadalcanal**. His victories there gave the momentum in the Pacific to the United States.

Halsey rose to commander of the Third Fleet and the Western Pacific Task Forces in 1944. He directed the first carrier attack against an inland enemy flight station in the Philippines and supported General **Douglas MacArthur**'s invasion of the islands (see no. 87).

His most controversial battle was in **Leyte Gulf** (1944). Halsey was lured away from the battle area by a decoy Japanese force. This allowed the main Japanese fleet to enter the gulf and attack the American ships there. Despite being drawn away, Halsey directed his planes in the attack and they sank four Japanese carriers. After this rocky start to the battle, the Americans won the most impressive naval victory of the war.

Halsey directed his fleet in the carrier attack on Okinawa, and his planes struck again and again at the Japanese mainland, including Tokyo. The Japanese surrender was conducted aboard his flagship, the ***USS Missouri***, although it was General MacArthur who led the U.S. delegation.

Promoted to fleet admiral in 1945, Halsey retired from the navy in 1947.

William Halsey, Jr.

89. Isoruku Yamamoto
(1884–1943)

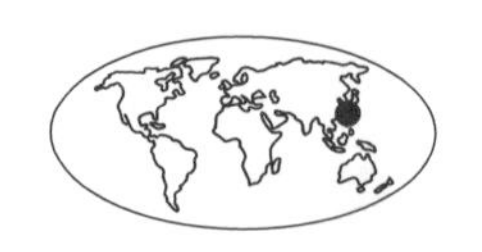

The sixth son of a school principal, **Isoruku Yamamoto** was born in Nagoaka, Honshu, Japan. He graduated from the Imperial Naval Academy in 1904 and entered the navy in time for the **Russo-Japanese War**. He was wounded in the critical **Battle of Tsushima Straits** (1905).

Yamamoto spent four years in the United States (1919–1921; 1925–1927) as a naval attaché. He recognized the awesome potential of American industry, but he believed that in a conflict the moral superiority of the Japanese would prevail. Yamamoto commanded the carrier *Akagi* (1928–1929) and was given command of Carrier Division One in 1933. He served as navy minister (1936–1938) and became chief of the Combined Fleet in 1939.

As war with the United States became more likely, Yamamoto pressed his fellow members of the Japanese high command to consider a preemptive strike. Believing that one swift blow would disable the American fleet and devastate American morale, he developed the plans for the surprise attack on **Pearl Harbor**.

Yamamoto's policy seemed vindicated at first. The attack on Pearl Harbor (December 7, 1941) was followed by the capture of the Philippines and the Japanese conquest of much of southeast Asia. Nervous, however, over the possibility of American bombardment of the Japanese mainland, Yamamoto decided on a second great attack that would eliminate the U.S. Navy from the Pacific Ocean.

Yamamoto left Japanese waters with the bulk of the navy in May 1942. Unaware that the Americans had just succeeded in breaking the Japanese communications code, Yamamoto steamed toward **Midway Island** to disperse the American ships there. Instead, he was met and attacked by two groups of American carriers sent to intercept him. The **Battle of Midway** (June 1942) could have gone either way, but at a crucial moment, American fighters caught hundreds of Japanese planes refueling on the decks of their carriers. Four Japanese carriers were lost that day, ending Japan's domination of the seas.

Isoruku Yamamoto

Although he knew his cause was now hopeless, Yamamoto continued the fight. He made a mistake in allowing Japan to be dragged into the fight for the island of **Guadalcanal**; precious Japanese resources were soon consumed by the battle. Yamamoto flew to the area to inspect the fight for the **Solomon Islands**, but he died when his plane was shot down by American fighters over the **Shortland Islands**. Brilliant and devoted to his nation's cause, Yamamoto had nevertheless made strategic errors that brought Japan to the brink of disaster by the time of his death.

90. Chester Nimitz
(1885–1966)

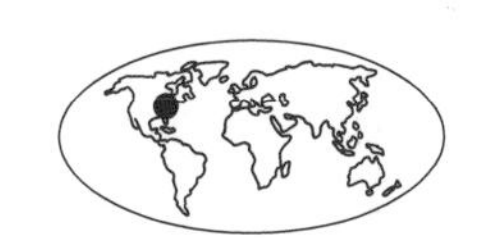

Chester Nimitz was born in Fredericksburg, Texas. Nimitz worked from the age of eight and wanted to attend the **U.S. Military Academy at West Point**. Failing to realize that goal, he went to the **U.S. Naval Academy at Annapolis** and graduated seventh in his class in 1905.

After two years of routine duty, Nimitz went to the Philippines and commanded the destroyer *USS Decatur*. His ship ran aground, and Nimitz was court-martialed and found guilty. Remarkably, he was let off with a reprimand, thereby saving the career of the future leader of the U.S. Navy.

After 1908, Nimitz specialized in the development and use of diesel engines. He was chief of staff to the Command Submarine Force of the U.S. Atlantic Fleet throughout **World War I**. During the long period between the two world wars, he became a rear admiral, commanded a battleship division, and became chief of the Naval Bureau of Navigation.

When **World War II** began, Nimitz was called to the office of the secretary of the navy. After consulting Nimitz on navigation matters, Secretary Knox was so impressed that he sent Nimitz to the Pacific as admiral of the Pacific Fleet. In 1942, Nimitz rose to the rank of commander-in-chief of the Pacific Ocean Areas. As such, he was the equal of two other high commanders in the war — **Dwight D. Eisenhower** and **Douglas MacArthur** (see no. 87).

Nimitz positioned his carrier fleet to take advantage of the Japanese attack at **Midway** in 1942. He won that desperate battle, sinking or disabling four Japanese carriers. In November 1943, he directed a new, shorter line of attack across the Pacific that caught the Japanese defenders flat-footed. He supported General MacArthur's invasion of the **Philippines** (1944) and was in overall command during the battles of **Pacific Sea** (June 1944) and **Leyte Gulf** (October 1944). His naval forces went on to capture **Iwo Jima** and **Okinawa** in 1945. Nimitz chose his subordinates with great care, and then gave them as much latitude as he could. He chose to allow his fleet commanders, **William Halsey** and **Raymond Spruance**, to conduct the battles. He did not want his presence to hinder their choices or initiative during the battles. Keeping watch over the fray, he stayed at his command stations, first at Pearl Harbor, and later on Guam.

Nimitz served as chief of naval operations from 1945 to 1947. He was later a goodwill ambassador for the **United Nations** (1949–1952), but never formally retired from the navy. He died at the naval station on Yerba Buena Island in San Francisco Bay.

Chester Nimitz

91. George Patton
(1885–1945)

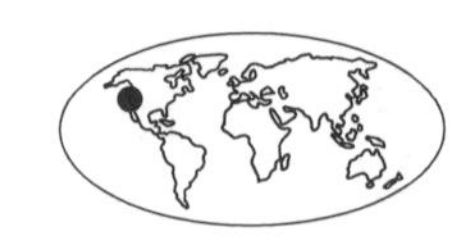

Born in San Gabriel, California, **George S. Patton, Jr.**, was the grandson of Confederate military leaders. He attended Virginia Military Institute before going to the **U.S. Military Academy at West Point**. He graduated in 1909 and was commissioned as a cavalry lieutenant. Patton's first chance to obtain recognition came when he served as aide to General **John Pershing** (see no. 85) in the chase after Mexican revolutionary **Pancho Villa**. Patton personally cornered and killed one of Villa's subordinates.

Patton went with Pershing to Europe in 1917 and served as the commanding officer of the general's headquarters. He also was one of the first officers named to enter the new tanks corps created late in **World War I**. Patton was wounded in the **Meuse-Argonne** offensive (1918).

As **World War II** approached, he was promoted to two-star general (1941). Patton was given command of the First Armored Corps. He played a prominent role in the Allied landings in **North Africa** in 1942. After the **Battle of Kasserine Pass**, he was made commander of the Second Armored Corps. Ordered to find a solution to the mobile warfare practiced by German general **Erwin Rommel** (see no. 94), Patton became a practitioner of the same art.

He led the Allied invasion that cleared the Germans from Sicily in 38 days, and he was near the height of his career when he brought criticism to himself after he slapped an American soldier in a hospital. The man was recovering from shell shock; Patton claimed he was malingering, but later issued an apology for his action.

Patton became commander of the Third Army in England (March 1944). He landed with his men at Normandy and led the famous "breakout" that equaled any of the German *blitzkrieg* campaigns in its audacity.

George Patton

Patton led his tanks and troops all the way to Nancy and Metz, bypassing Paris, before running out of gas and supplies.

During the **Battle of the Bulge** (December 1944), Patton raced northward with the Third Army, relieved the key city of **Bastogne**, and doomed the German offensive. Patton's troops crossed the Rhine River in March 1945, and he entered Czechoslovakia by the time the war ended.

Named military governor of Bavaria, Patton proved completely unsuited to such an administrative post. He openly preferred the Germans to the Soviets and hinted he would like to campaign against Russia in the future. Due to these intemperate statements, he was removed from command of the Third Army that October. Patton died in Heidelberg, Germany after an auto accident later that year.

92. Chiang Kai-shek
(1887–1975)

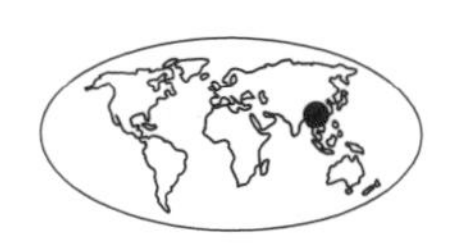

Chiang Kai-shek, the man who finally lost China to the Communists was born in Chikou, the son of a salt merchant who had built a modest fortune. He was educated at the government military college at Paoting. Chiang spent the years from 1907 to 1911 in Japan, training with the efficient Japanese military that had established its reputation in the **Russo-Japanese War**.

In 1911, Chiang joined the forces of revolution and reform in China. He fought in **Shanghai** during the conflict that led to the end of the **Manchu Dynasty**. He supported the new republican government founded in 1911, and in 1918, he joined the **Kuomintang**, the revolutionary government led by **Sun Yat-Sen**.

Chiang studied military tactics in Russia during 1923. He returned to China determined to reform the **Nationalist** army along the lines of the Soviet army. He directed the Whampoa Military Academy in 1924, and after the death of Sun Yat-Sen in 1925, he became commander of the northern expeditionary forces. Chiang's assignment was to subdue the five major warlords who dominated northern China.

Chiang carried out a military coup on March 20, 1926, against the **Chinese Communists** who had previously cooperated with the Kuomintang. He then went north and captured **Peking** in 1928.

In 1930, Chiang undertook heroic efforts to destroy what he saw as the greatest threat to China — the Communists within. Five times he tried to encircle them in their strongholds in the Jin Giang Mountains of southern China. In late 1933, he assembled a 700,000-man army. Using methods learned from a German advisor, he harried the Communists so effectively that they gave up their positions and undertook the "**Long March**" to safety in the north.

Chiang soon faced another threat, this one from Japan. The Japanese invaded China in 1937 and overran large sections of territory along the coast. Chiang and the Nationalists held out during the long period of Japanese ascendancy. Only the entry of the United States into **World War II** brought effective relief and the prospect of final success. Chiang remained commander-in-chief of the Nationalists throughout the war.

After World War II ended, Chiang again went to war with the Chinese Communists. He lost the battle in the countryside, where millions of peasants heard more hope in the messages of **Mao Zedong** (see no. 95) than in Chiang's. He resigned as president in January 1949 and fled to the island of **Taiwan**. Soon resuming his presidency, Chiang became head of the Chinese national government in exile. The **United Nations** recognition of mainland China in 1972 was a bitter blow to Chiang and the Nationalists he led. He died in Taipei.

Chiang Kai-shek (*left*)

93. Heinz Guderian
(1888–1954)

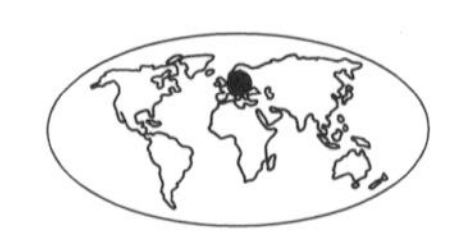

Little is known of the early years of Germany's foremost advocate of *blitzkrieg* warfare. **Heinz Guderian** was born in Kulm, Germany (present-day Chelmno, Poland). He was commissioned into a Hanoverian rifle battalion in 1908 and then transferred to become a communications officer. He commanded a radio station during **World War I**.

After the war ended, Guderian became deeply involved in the rebuilding of the German military. Convinced that motorized vehicles would bring about great changes in warfare, he called for changes in tactics. Guderian especially believed that the static trench warfare of World War I would soon be obsolete.

In 1931, Guderian was given command of a motorized battalion. When three German *panzer* (tank) divisions were created in 1935, Guderian was named to command one. He also found time to write a book, *Achtung! Panzer!*, during 1936 and 1937. Guderian became chief of all mobile German troops in 1938.

At the start of **World War II**, most European planners anticipated a long, drawn-out war. Instead, the lightning speed of the German armored units stunned the Poles, and Germany conquered Poland in only six weeks. This success proved Guderian's military philosophy, and he was given the task of planning the coming campaign against France. It also confirmed his key motto: *"Klotzern, nicht kleckern"* ("Smash, don't tap").

Guderian himself led an army corps into France in the spring of 1940. The stunning German successes there were even greater than he had hoped for, and his nervous superiors back in Berlin became anxious that he might exceed his directives. Hitler himself called a halt to the offensive a short distance from Dunkirk, where they might have destroyed the British army before it was evac-

Heinz Guderian

uated from the continent. By this time, Guderian was called "**Father of the Panzer Divisions.**"

In 1941, Guderian commanded the Second *Panzerarmee* (tank army) in its thrust into Russia; he gained immense victories by isolating and enveloping Russian forces. However, he had reached his high-water mark; Hitler replaced him in December 1941 for withdrawing without confirmation of his intentions from Berlin.

Guderian passed an uneventful two-and-a-half years before he was summoned to serve as chief of the army general staff (July 1944–March 1945). In the melee that followed the breakdown of the German eastern front, Guderian was again summarily replaced by Hitler.

Although he was complicit in the arrest and shooting of many Soviet Red Army prisoners, contrary to the Geneva agreements, Guderian was never brought to trial. He died near Fussen, Bavaria.

94. Erwin Rommel
(1891–1944)

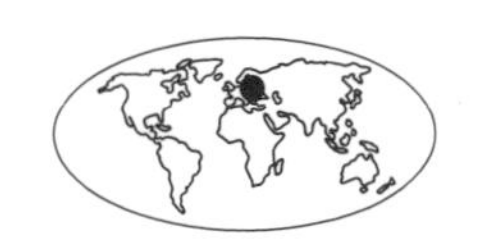

Erwin Rommel personified chivalry and courage in an age of warfare that was generally characterized by brutality. He was born in Heidenheim, Wurttemberg, and joined the German infantry as an officer cadet in 1910. Commissioned a second lieutenant in 1912, he served in France, Romania and Italy during **World War I**.

Rommel was a military instructor at the Dresden Infantry School (1929–1933) and Potsdam War Academy (1935–1938). Still a junior officer, he first came to prominence when he was given responsibility for **Adolf Hitler**'s safety during Hitler's triumphal ride through Prague in 1938. Rommel held this duty again during the German invasion of Poland in 1939.

Promoted to major general on the eve of **World War II**, Rommel commanded the 7th Panzer Division in the invasion of France in 1940. His brilliance as a battlefield leader was recognized by Hitler, and in 1941, Rommel was sent to Libya to command the German-Italian forces there.

During two years in North Africa (1941–1943), Rommel fought against numerically superior forces, dealt with his inadequate supply lines (especially after the British used Malta as an air base), and received conflicting orders from Berlin. Using his personal magnetism to infuse his troops with hope and drive, he outmaneuvered and defeated the British several times, finally capturing **Tobruk** in 1942. His string of successes came to an end at **El Alamein**, where he was defeated by General **Bernard Montgomery** (see no. 86) of England.

Recalled to Germany in 1943, Rommel was given command of all German forces from the Netherlands to the Loire River. He worked ceaselessly to fortify the French coast against an Allied invasion but knew the tremendous odds against him. When the Allied **D-Day invasion** came in Normandy on June 6, 1944, Rommel had two armored units close at hand. However, he was unable to use them until four o'clock in the afternoon, when they were given permission by Hitler's phone call. By then it was too late; the Allies had come ashore to stay.

Hoping against hope, Rommel fought on for a month before he was wounded by Allied aircraft fire while in his automobile. Taken to Berlin, he was implicated in the effort to remove Hitler from power. On October 14, 1944, he was visited at his home by two generals who offered him a choice: he could either take poison and remain a great hero, or he could take his chance with a "People's Trial." Rommel made his choice, took poison, and died to protect his family. The Nazi government pretended he had died from his wounds, and Hitler announced a day of national mourning for the fallen hero.

Erwin Rommel

95. Mao Zedong (Mao Tse-Tung)
(1893–1976)

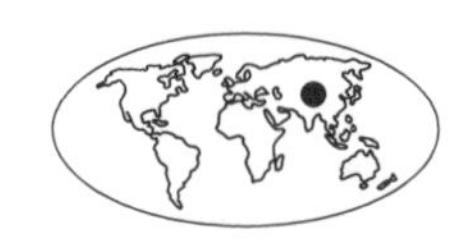

The leader of the Chinese Communist Party, **Mao Zedong** won the **Chinese Civil War.** His truly drastic policies decisively shaped China during the 20th century. During his youth and adolescence, China had thrown off the rule of the **Manchu** (Ch'ing) **Dynasty** and created a republic.

Mao joined the **Chinese Marxist Party** in 1920. He and 11 others founded the **Chinese Communist Party** in 1921. For several years, Mao and his followers cooperated with the **Chinese Nationalists,** led by General **Chiang Kai-shek** (see no. 92). In 1927, Chiang carried out a sudden coup against the Communists. Mao quickly became a military leader out of necessity. For the next 22 years, Mao would focus on rural China and the common peasants as the bulwark of the Communist Party.

Mao commanded perhaps 10,000 men in 1928, but by the early 1930s, that figure had risen to nearly 300,000. However, Mao and his followers were under constant attack from Chiang's Nationalist forces.

Mao's response was to initiate and lead the "**Long March.**" Commencing on October 16, 1934, Mao led 86,000 Chinese Communists on a daring, apparently suicidal, retreat from the Jin Giang Mountains north through the Hunan, Kweichow, and Szechwan provinces. The Communists crossed 18 mountain ranges — six of them snow-covered — 24 rivers, and vast swamps on their march north. They also eluded Chiang's forces. It is believed that only 4,000 of the original 86,000 troops reached their destination in northern Shensai province in October 1935; many others dropped out along the way. However, the march brought national and international attention to the Communists, and their numbers were soon swollen by recruits. The epic journey made Mao the indelible leader of Chinese Communism.

Mao

Mao stayed on the sidelines during the **Sino-Japanese War** (1937–1945). He perceived Chiang and the Nationalists as his true enemy. After the conclusion of **World War II,** and the eviction of the Japanese from China, the Communists and Nationalists continued their conflict. Chiang and the Nationalists held on to the cities, but Mao and the Communists gained control of the entire countryside. Chiang fled to **Taiwan**, and in 1949, Mao marched into **Peking** as the leader of a new Communist nation.

Mao led China through the "**Cold War.**" He signed a treaty with the Soviet Union in 1950 and sent his troops across the Yalu River into the **Korean War** later that year.

Mao directed the start of the "**Great Leap Forward**" (1958) and the **Cultural Revolution** (1966–1969). He reversed an old policy in 1971 and welcomed President **Richard Nixon** of the United States to China. At the time of his death, Mao was the most revered leader in the Communist world.

96. Georgi Zhukov
(1896–1974)

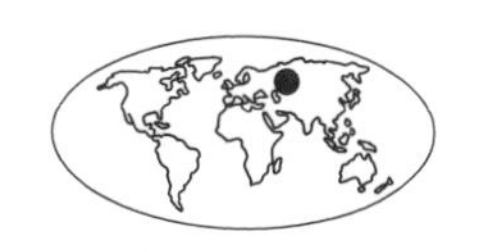

Georgi Zhukov was born in a village in Kaluga Province, southwest of Moscow. He joined the Novgorad dragoons in 1915, rose to sergeant, and twice received the St. George's Cross.

After learning military tactics in the Czar's army, Zhukov joined the new **Red Army** when the **Bolshevik Revolution** brought down the czar. He advanced rapidly in the Communist forces, rising to squadron commander by 1922. Zhukov attended the Frunze Military Academy from 1928 to 1931, commanded a division of troops by 1934, and advanced to corps commander in 1936.

Zhukov managed to avoid the terrible purges carried out by **Joseph Stalin** during the late 1930s. He was sent east in 1939 to meet a threat from Japan. Zhukov planned and carried out a brilliant battle strategy that cost the Japanese 60,000 casualties in the **Khalkin-Gol** campaign. He thereby ensured that Russia's eastern front would remain quiet throughout most of **World War II**. He became chief of staff of the **Soviet Army** in 1940 and was made a full general the same year.

Zhukov played an active role in retraining and reshaping the Soviet Army after its deficiencies were shown in the **Russo-Finnish War** of 1939 and 1940. Like Stalin, Zhukov was lulled to sleep as far as the Germans were concerned; the Nazi invasion of Russia in June 1941 took him thoroughly by surprise.

As Russia fought for survival against the German invaders, Zhukov played increasingly larger roles. He commanded the defense of the central and **Leningrad** fronts in 1941, and organized the reserve units that stopped the Germans just short of **Moscow** in December 1941. Zhukov received the title of first deputy commissar for defense, meaning that after Premier Stalin, he was the overall commander of the Soviet war effort. Zhukov organized, though he did not carry out the counterattack at **Stalingrad** in 1942, and he was prominent in the relief of Leningrad. Made a full marshal of the Soviet Union, he led the troops that captured **Berlin** in April 1945, thereby ending the war.

Zhukov served as deputy minister of defense in 1946, but was relieved suddenly by Stalin. Sent to an obscure post at Odessa, he languished in semi-retirement until he was reinstated in 1952. He played an important part in ensuring that **Nikita Kruschev** came to power in 1955, but he was ousted by the premier in October 1957. The greatest Russian leader during the **Great Patrioic War** (the Russian name for World War II), Zhukov showed how a humble peasant could rise and fall under the Soviet system.

Georgi Zhukov

97. Vo Nguyen Giap
(b. 1912)

Vo Nguyen Giap was born in An Xa village in Quanbinh Province, **Vietnam.** Coming from an impoverished Mandarin family, he studied at a French school and earned a law degree from Hanoi University.

He joined to the Communist-Nationalist group led by **Ho Chi Minh** around 1930 and became one of its "inner circle" members. Giap joined Ho Chi Minh in China during **World War II.**

He then returned to Vietnam and organized a revolutionary army in the northern highlands. Determined to push out the French, he called for a massive insurrection.

The Vietnamese revolution succeeded in part. The Communists held the highland areas, but the French clung to at least half the country. As leader of the Vietnamese army, and later as defense minister from 1954 to 1980, Giap refined the guerrilla war principles he had learned in China.

Giap directed major attacks against the French in 1950. The Communists gained considerable ground, but the French regained most of the lost areas in counterattacks in 1951.

Giap then set a trap. It took three years for him to lure the French into committing the cream of their army to an exposed region, the fortress of **Dien Bien Phu.** Giap directed 100,000 peasants in movements that brought howitzers and mortars to the area. He assembled a massive **Vietnamese army** and commenced the siege on March 12, 1954. When Dien Bien Phu surrendered, it broke the back of French resistance.

The hero of the revolution against the French, Giap soon had to confront the democratic government in **South Vietnam,** one that was supported by the power of the United States. Giap directed the **North Vietnamese** troops during the long war from 1963 to 1975. It is unclear whether the idea for the **Tet offensive** in 1968 was initially his own, but his reputation as a soldier stood behind it. Although the North Vietnamese lost thousands of lives throwing themselves against South Vietnamese and American installations, the overall effect was to lower the willingness of many Americans to continue the war.

Vo Nguyen Giap

By the time the **Vietnam War** ended in 1975, with the American troops in flight, much of the direction of the war had passed to General **Van Tien Dung.** Giap remained the grand old man of the Vietnam military. He had good reason to be proud. His poorly equipped guerrilla warriors had defeated France, South Vietnam and the United States in a protracted struggle of more than 30 years.

98. Benjamin O. Davis, Jr.
(b. 1912)

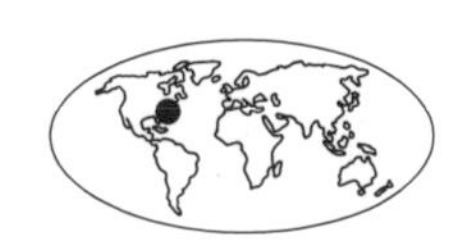

Born in Washington, D.C., **Benjamin O. Davis, Jr.** was the son of a military officer who, in 1940, became the first African-American to achieve the rank of general.

Davis, Jr., attended the University of Chicago before going to the **U.S. Military Academy at West Point**. Because he suffered the "silent treatment" there, none of his classmates roomed or ate with him, and he was never spoken to unless it was an order. Davis graduated 35 out of a class of 276 in 1936. His high placement allowed him to select the service of his choice, and he chose the air force. However, he was told that African-Americans could not serve as fighter pilots.

Commissioned in the infantry, Davis taught military science at the Tuskegee Institute. He endured segregation in the bases he was assigned to: Fort Benning, Georgia and Fort Riley, Kansas. In 1941, Davis was a member of the first group of African-Americans admitted to the U.S. Army Air Corps and pilot training. Davis organized the all-black **99th Pursuit Squadron** in 1942 and flew missions over North Africa, Sicily and Italy. They became known as the "**Tuskegee Airmen.**"

Davis went on to organize the **332nd Fighter Group** in 1943, composed of four black squadrons. Promoted to full colonel, Davis flew missions over Germany.

Davis followed his distinguished **World War II** service by commanding fighter fields in the United States. The desegregation of the Armed Forces removed his last stumbling block, and he surged ahead, graduating from the Air War College in 1950. As chief of the fighter branch, he commanded the **51st Fighter Interceptor Wing** in Korea (1953–1954). Raised to brigadier general in 1954, and to major general in 1959, Davis served for two years in Europe before returning to the United States for a tour of duty in Washington, D.C. (1961–1965).

Davis became the first African-American promoted to lieutenant general (1965), and he served as chief of staff of the U.S. forces in Korea from 1965 to 1968. At the time of his retirement from the service in 1970, he was the senior African-American officer in the U.S. armed forces. He later served as assistant secretary of transportation (1971–1975), where he argued passionately for the 55 mile-per-hour speed limit on interstate highways to save both lives and fuel.

Davis was a remarkable individual who chose to ignore the prejudice and insults directed against him. He strongly objected to being classified as "African-American" since he believed that "we are all simply American."

Benjamin O. Davis, Jr.

99. Moshe Dayan
(1915–1981)

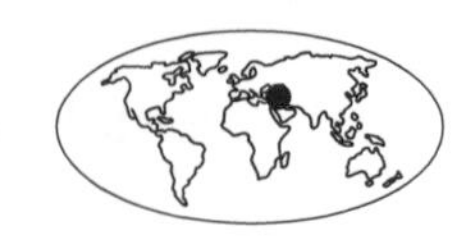

One of the true military geniuses of the 20th century, **Moshe Dayan** was born in Daganyah A, the first Jewish collaborative settlement in **Palestine** (modern-day Israel). At the age of 14, he joined the ***Haganah***, the Jewish militia that operated in British-administered Palestine. During the **Palestine-Arab Revolt** of 1936 to 1939, Dayan led special night squadrons to protect British military installations and Jewish settlements.

The Haganah went underground in 1939 after British policy appeared to favor Arab control of Palestine. Dayan was caught by the British and sentenced to a five-year prison term, but was released in 1941. He then joined British and Free French troops in their campaign to liberate Syria and Lebanon from the control of Vichy France, which had joined the Nazis in 1940. Dayan lost his right eye in this conflict; he soon took to wearing the large, black eye patch that became his personal trademark.

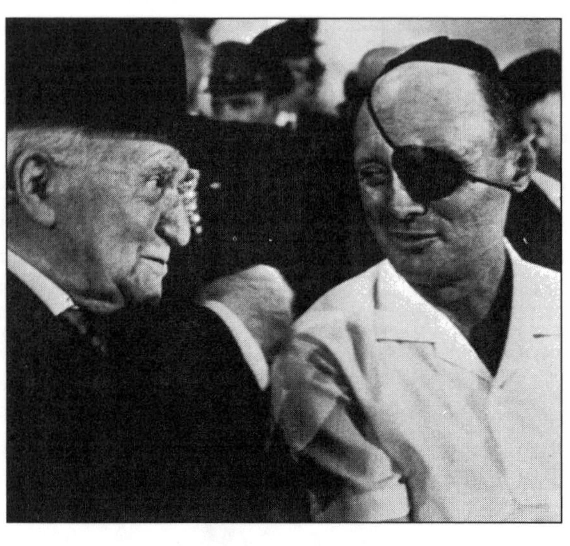

Moshe Dayan (*right*) with David Ben-Gurion

When the Israeli war for independence began in 1948, Dayan commanded a battalion on the Syrian front. By the end of the war in 1949, he had risen to command of the **Jerusalem** front, thereby gaining an intimate knowledge of the vital geographic points of the **new Jewish state.**

Dayan received military training in Britain after the war. He returned to Israel and became chief of the general staff in 1953. He was supreme commander of the **Israeli Defense Forces** during the 1956 war against Egypt, and fought in the **Sinai Desert**. By this time, the Israelis had gained an edge over the Arabs in both skill and weaponry. Dayan's victory in the war confirmed Israel's position as a new military power.

Dayan left the army in 1958 and studied politics before he won a seat in the ***Knesset***, Israel's parliament. A member of the Labor Party, he served as minister of agriculture (1959–1964). When the Israeli government organized a united coalition cabinet just prior to war in 1967, he was made minister of defense.

The **Six Day War** in June 1967 vindicated everything Dayan had worked toward for more than 30 years. The Israeli air force destroyed Arab planes on the ground; Israeli soldiers seized the **Golan Heights**, liberated Jerusalem, and captured the **Sinai peninsula.** The stunning victory was attributed to Israeli preparedness, which in no small measure was due to Dayan's vigilance and forethought.

Dayan was replaced as defense minister in 1974. He suffered criticism over Israel's lack of preparedness for the **Yom Kippur War** in 1973. He returned to politics to serve as foeign minister (1977–1979), an exciting time during which Israeli and Egyptian leaders laid the basis for peace between their two countries.

100. Norman Schwarzkopf (b. 1934)

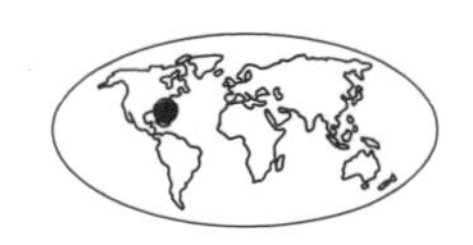

Norman Schwarzkopf was born in Trenton, New Jersey. His father was a brigadier general and had headed the investigation of the famous Lindbergh kidnapping case. Young Schwarzkopf graduated 43rd out of his class of 480 at the **U.S. Military Academy at West Point** and served for two years with the 101st Airborne Division.

Schwarzkopf served in Berlin for two years before returning to West Point as an instructor. The start of the **Vietnam War** changed his plans; he went to serve as a task-force advisor to a South Vietnamese airborne division in 1965. In all, Schwarzkopf served three tours of duty in Vietnam and won three Silver Stars. His most famous incident came on May 28, 1970, when he chose to be landed in a mine field and lead a group of his men to safety. His devotion to his men, as well as his high temper and self-assurance, led many soldiers to call him "**Stormin' Norman.**"

As commander-in-chief of the United States Central Command, Schwarzkopf was the natural choice to lead the war against Iraq (1990–1991). After Iraqi dictator **Saddam Hussein** invaded and seized oil-rich Kuwait, Schwarzkopf was sent to Saudi Arabia to command **Operation Desert Shield.**

Welding together a coalition of allied forces from European, Middle Eastern and North American countries, Schwarzkopf laid the groundwork for the invasion of Kuwait and the ejection of Iraqi troops. After a month of fierce aerial bombardment that failed to persuade Hussein to withdraw, Schwarzkopf was given the green light to unleash **Operation Desert Storm**. The campaign lasted approximately 100 hours, from February 23 to February 27, 1991. Schwarzkopf's meticulous preparation paid off as his coalition forces outflanked, outfought and routed the Iraqi army. When a cease-fire was called on February 27, Schwarzkopf had not only liberated Kuwait, but he stood in a position to push all the way to Baghdad and remove Saddam Hussein from power.

That was not to be the case. President **George Bush** of the U.S. and head of the Joint Chiefs of Staff **Colin Powell** declared themselves satisfied that the **United Nations**' objectives had been attained. The war ended, with Kuwait freed and Hussein corralled, but still in power in Iraq.

Schwarzkopf returned home a hero. He addressed both houses of the U.S. Congress and led a ticker-tape parade in New York City. He received an honorary knighthood from Queen **Elizabeth II** of England. Mentioned by some as a possible candidate for president in 1992, Schwarzkopf dismissed such talk as rumors. Instead he embarked on a promotional tour for his best-selling book, *It Doesn't Take a Hero* (1992).

Norman Schwarzkopf

TRIVIA QUIZ

Test your knowledge and challenge your friends with the following questions. The answers are on the biographies noted.

1.What is the difference between Yoshimotto, *Yamoto* and Yamamoto? (see nos. 46, 82, 89)

2.Which feared warrior developed a disciplined system of force that used mobile horse columns to encircle and entrap enemies who were then killed using armor-piercing arrows? (see no. 30)

3.What did legend say about the man who could untie the Gordian Knot? Who succeeded in this task and how? (see no. 6)

4.Who removed his half-sister from power by banishing her to a convent in order to become czar of Russia? (see no. 56)

5.Who was the peasant girl that became a warrior and saved the French monarchy from England after she had visions of such a destiny? (see no. 39)

6.Which military leader was not only a great European warrior but was also a promoter of cultural enrichment, helping to bring about the "Carolingian Renaissance"? (see no. 20)

7.Who was the first African-American promoted to the rank of lieutenant general? (see no. 98)

8.What was the Committee of Public Safety most notorious for during the French Revolution? (see no. 65)

9.Several military leaders fought for land from which they were later banished. Can you name them and their homelands? (see nos. 64, 65, 67, 79, 80, 92)

10. Who introduced the use of ricochet gunfire? Describe that method of battle. (see no. 54)

11. This freedom fighter was known as the "George Washington of South America" and this one was known as the "father of his country." Name these leaders. (see nos. 62 and 70)

12. Whose death on the Plains of Abraham was commemorated in a painting by Benjamin West? (see no. 60)

13. How did "Stonewall" Jackson get his nickname? Why is that ironic? (see no. 78)

14. Which famous military leader and president of the United States sold his swords and souvenirs for money during the poverty-stricken later years of his life? (see no. 76)

15. Describe the "Long March." Who was its leader and what effect did it have on Communism? (see no. 95)

SUGGESTED PROJECTS

1. Niccolo Machiavelli once declared, "[W]ar and its organization and discipline ... is the only art that is necessary to one who commands." Which wars strike you as having been particularly well organized? Make a list of the wars and then name the military leaders involved.

2. Some of the military leaders in this book have been memorialized in poems. For example, a great epic poem was written about El Cid, Charlemagne's grief over the loss of Roland and his knights was described in "The Song of Roland," and Robert Bruce was the subject of a poem by John Barbour. Select one of the leaders in this book and write your own poem about his or her adventures.

INDEX

INDEX

INDEX

INDEX